Praise for *I Am with You Everywhere*

This book is a heartwarming and heartbreaking tribute to a remarkable woman written by her equally remarkable mother. Most importantly, this is a wonderful example of healthy grief through nurturing the living bond that exists with our loved ones long after they leave our physical world as they continue to impact all who knew them. This living bond grows stronger and more resolute with time, providing support and comfort. This is a well-written, funny, poignant story that honours a truly unique Canadian life and demonstrates the remarkable resilience of spirit and family.

~ Debbie McAllister, MSc, MD, FRCPC Anesthesia, FRCPC Palliative Care Medicine. Clinical Associate Professor Cumming School of Medicine, University of Calgary

The beguiling first chapters of her book depict a warm-hearted family life, which ended abruptly when their daughter, Siu-Ling, was diagnosed with ovarian cancer.

Kim Han shares a parent's worst experience in simple, powerful language. Acknowledging her own heartache, she examines various techniques for climbing out of the abyss of raw pain and grief. Despite the subject, this is an uplifting read.

~ Madeleine McDonald, Author, *A Shackled Inheritance*

Grief. Love. Loss. Healing. Stillness. Movement. I feel honored to be able to read this amazing book. Deep feelings about love and loss, heartbreak and healing came pouring in. I laughed, cried, and felt incredible love and energy course through me while I read. I felt Siu-Ling hold me and comfort me, telling me everything was alright.

In I Am with You Everywhere: Finding Solace in the Mists of Grief, *we are invited into Kim's home and life and are well cared for as visitors, feeling and healing alongside her. I feel more connected, somehow, to everything and everyone. I am more present with my own grief and can better receive my lessons on life. Thank you, Kim for sharing this most intimate offering, I am so appreciative of this gift.*

~ Michael Overlie, Canine-Partnered Energy Coach, Energy Healer and Author of *Let Your Dog Lead.*

Kim Han shares her deeply personal and touching story of her daughter's life before and after her passing at the age of 53 from ovarian cancer. A brand of grief that only a parent can know, she shows how she navigated this difficult passage to "ease the ragged edges of a broken heart." Kim opens to the inspiration that her daughter's life provided her and shares how she eventually found meaning in the loss. An inspiring story that reminds us that love truly never dies.

~ Pam Culley-McCullough, Ed.D. Author of *The Promise of Soul Love, Unexpected Gifts from Here and Beyond*

I Am with You Everywhere: Finding Solace in the Mists of Grief *is not only a beautiful tribute to Kim's beloved daughter Siu-Ling, but such an honest and vulnerable sharing of what a mother goes through when she loses a child. Through Kim's story, those experiencing grief will see someone else who has experienced the deepest levels of sadness and despair and has managed to keep moving forward and find moments of joy and peace. Kim's book offers hope as she shares many different strategies that helped her, and she is so encouraging to others going through grief, letting them know that they too can get through this. All of these strategies are not only supported by research, but I have seen them help my clients who are experiencing grief in my coaching practice.*

~ Patricia Barrett-Robillard, RN, BScN, MNRS
Cancer Coach at the Ottawa Regional Cancer Foundation

I have come to realize through multiple experiences that when one transitions from bodily form, the Love and Light that is true and ever-present lives on everywhere. Kim Han, in this precious account of her daughter's adventurous and love-filled life and passing, is testament to that realization. Your journey through Kim's story with her beloved Siu-Ling will inspire you to realize there is indeed solace and peace in the mists of grief. Siu-Ling's and Kim's sense of adventure, courage, and deep love jump off every page and have stayed with me since having the pleasure of experiencing this beautiful book.

~ Rev. Cathy Silva, Author, Coach and Founder of Live Your Life
in Love Ministry

This is an exquisite love story...that of a mother for her dying daughter and the journey through shattered hearts to wholeness. Prepare to go deep within yourself as you witness the twists and turns of dying too young and how a mother finds her way forward. Tears will flow as your heart is renewed by the power of love in this lifetime...and beyond. This is a book you don't want to miss.

~ Dr. Kymn Harvin, author of *The Soul of America Speaks: Wisdom for Healing and Moving Forward*

A mother writes with love about her daughter. Perhaps inevitably, the result is elegantly poetic.

There is a man best known for his account of The Legend of John Hornby, *surely one of the North's greatest, albeit tragic, stories. In his day job, George Whalley was a university professor of English whose 1953 book* Poetic Process *describes "symbolic extrication" as the means by which the writer releases herself from "an intolerable reality." This is what Kim Han seeks with her new book, while "finding solace in the mists of grief." Poetry is the language of love; without doubt, this is Kim Han's love poem to her daughter.*

Losing a child is an insufferable pain; few of us can really understand this. I do; that we share, this mother and I, though we have never met. I celebrate the effort Kim Han makes here to confront her loss, to give Siu-Ling's life greater meaning, and to impart to others the lesson that love never dies. It is a very, very personal story – for some, perhaps almost too much to bear – but it will not fail to inspire you to contemplate the sheer joy of life.

~ David F. Pelly, author of *The Ancestors Are Happy* and several other books about the North, the land, its people, and their history. www.DavidPelly.com
Co-Founder of the Ayalik Fund, a charitable initiative to support Inuit youth. www.AyalikFund.ca

Siu-Ling's story of outdoor adventures and Inuit history in the North and music and far-flung travel—and yes, of her dying—lifts us above the mists of gloom and grief into a place of peace and promise—and continuing connection.
  ~ Linda Bryce, MA, author of the bestseller, *The Courage to Care: Being Fully Present with the Dying.*

Kim Han's book is an inspiring tribute to her daughter, Siu-Ling, and how she lived an extraordinary life both before and after her cancer diagnosis. She loved the outdoors and continued doing many things that brought her joy, including skiing, hiking, wilderness camping and dogsledding, which helped her to live another 13 years after her diagnosis. Even though Siu-Ling has passed, her story is a wonderful reminder to fully embrace life and living, no matter what challenges you may be facing.
  ~ Leslie Bridger, author of *Alive and Thriving: Miraculous Healing Above and Beyond the Odds*

With tenderness and strength, author and grieving mother Kim Han takes the reader through the life and death of her daughter, Siu-Ling, who died of cancer at 53 in 2016. In I Am with You Everywhere, *Han talks about how she survived the loss of her daughter, who was an accomplished researcher, dog team musher, singer, songwriter, and friend, and she shares that hard-earned knowledge in this book.*
  ~ Jane George, longtime northern journalist and
    friend of Siu-Ling

As a person who has been through loss and grief of my own, I have been totally moved from tears to inspiration by Kim Han's wonderful book: I Am with You Everywhere - Finding Solace in the Mists of Grief. *I am so uplifted and inspired by the wisdom and amazingness of Siu-Ling, powerfully and lovingly shared by her mother, and by Kim's journey through her own grief, which enabled her to bring us this transformational and uplifting book that has certainly helped me. I will be happy and grateful to share this book with my clients, friends, and colleagues.*

~ Gary Nobuo Niki, Shamanic Samurai Medicine Man, DIY Zen Guy and Author of *d.i.y. zen and The Art of Gentle Emotional Transformation*
www.GaryNiki.com

I Am with You Everywhere

FINDING SOLACE
IN THE MISTS OF GRIEF

KIM HAN

Capucia LLC
211 Pauline Drive #513
York, PA 17402
www.capuciapublishing.com
Send questions to: support@capuciapublishing.com

Paperback ISBN: 978-1-954920-32-3
eBook ISBN: 978-1-954920-33-0
Library of Congress Control Number: 2022912808

Cover Design: Ranilo Cabo
Layout: Ranilo Cabo
Editor and Proofreader: Susan Bruck
Book Midwife: Karen Everitt

Printed in the United States of America

Capucia LLC is proud to be a part of the Tree Neutral® program. Tree Neutral offsets the number of trees consumed in the production and printing of this book by taking proactive steps such as planting trees in direct proportion to the number of trees used to print books. To learn more about Tree Neutral, please visit treeneutral.com.

All proceeds from the sale of this book will be donated to the Ilisaqsivik Society, a community-led, not-for-profit Inuit organization in Clyde River that offers Inuit-led, culturally and linguistically relevant community programs and counselling services for its residents and others in Nunavut. Ilisaqsivik supports the physical, emotional, spiritual and mental well-being of individuals through every stage of life to create thriving, sustainable communities. Its programs and services are based on *Inuit Qaujimajatuqangit* (traditional knowledge) and *Inuuqatigiitiarniq* (the healthy interconnection of mind, body, spirit, and the environment as a path to healing.)

This book is dedicated to my much-loved daughter, Siu-Ling, who was an inspiration, a guiding light, and a pillar of strength to our family. It honors her love and respect for nature, Canada's Arctic, its people, environment, and wildlife, and her dedication to making this world a little better.

Also, to my family and to all who loved, admired, and cared about Siu-Ling.

CONTENTS

FOREWORD

Blending memoir with personal and professional insights into how to live with loss, Kim Han honors her beautiful daughter Siu Ling and, in the process, gently offers readers tools for coping. Kim takes us around the world, up mountains, through forests, and across the tundra of her memories.

Sharing our pain with caring people and receiving love, and empathy, and solidarity in return can lessen the burden of loss whether it be the death of a loved one, a dream let go, or an imagined future that is no longer possible. For complicated or disenfranchised grief in particular, seeking professional care and support can be therapeutic, and it is even more vital not to suffer alone.

There are few more universal human experiences, however. In addition to our own birth and death, the experience of grief and loss comes to us all eventually. Kim writes about the healing powers of nature, exercise, writing, friendship, social connectedness, service, and more.

Cry, wail, laugh, shout. Feel the feelings. Be gentle with yourself. Expect with time that grief will change, and the balance will eventually shift to more joy and less pain. There must be movement around the monument of grief. Like a monument - or a tree or a mountain, for that matter - our grief will appear and be felt differently depending on our changing perspective, the light, and the season.

Dr. Madeleine Cole MD CCFP FCFP
Clinical Assistant Professor, Discipline of Family Medicine,
Memorial University of Newfoundland
Assistant Professor, Department of Family Medicine
University of Ottawa

INTRODUCTION

This book celebrates my love for my daughter, Siu-Ling, who we lost to cancer in 2016, when she was only 53 years old. Siu-Ling was our guiding light and the rock in our family. Her brothers called her "the wise one" because she was a problem solver and knew so much about so many things. Siu-Ling was an inspiration; she endeavored to make this world a better place as an environmentalist, wildlife manager, friend, and colleague. I would not have written this book if she still had been with us. I would give anything to still have my daughter with me, but that was not a choice I was given. I tried to find meaning in this tremendous loss, but all I found were sadness and tears.

Sometimes, even in the mists of grief, the universe sends us a gift, something beyond our expectations or control, that changes the world once again. I received such an unexpected gift the day I was surfing the Internet and somehow came upon a video of Christine Kloser on a beach in the Bahamas, where she was hosting a writing retreat. Against the serene backdrop of the blue Atlantic Ocean, the lovely lady in the video talking about how to get your book written caught my attention. She had an open and friendly face that shone with sincerity and enthusiasm. Before I knew it, I decided to participate in her Breakthrough Event in York, PA, in October 2018 and, maybe, if all went well, write a book.

When I first met Christine in person, I felt such a strong spark of connection, or recognition, that I almost choked with emotion. I never felt that way before with someone I met for the first time. Something about Christine made me feel the warm embrace of spiritual connection.

During Christine's workshop, there were moments when the atmosphere tugged at my heartstrings and brought tears to my eyes. I suddenly felt a strong urge to write about my feelings that were bubbling to the surface. There are no words to describe the pain of losing my beloved child and the grief that almost consumed me, and I realized that I could not go on holding all those feelings in.

My mind flashed back to a time of sunshine, life, love, and laughter, a time when Siu-Ling was still with us. Those memories broke through the nagging pain of my grief to soothe my broken heart. A title for a book popped into my mind, "Finding Solace in the Mists of Grief." I did not know how to find that solace, but I was determined to find it and rise above my grief, to find sunshine, embrace life, and relish love and laughter once again. Siu-Ling would want that for me.

As, during a writing exercise, I pondered how to begin my book, something Siu-Ling said to me before she passed away struck me. Those words became the opening words to my book as I reflected on an event in my life that is as clear today as it was more than fifty years ago when it happened. It was as if a light went on as the meaning of that life-altering event started dawning on me. Putting my thoughts and feelings into words has been an emotional roller coaster. Still, I managed to muddle through with help and guidance from Christine Kloser and her wonderful team and the encouragement of my family and friends.

It took me more than a year to write this book through the ups and downs of my daily life. There were times when I could not get myself together to write anything at all. But as January 22, 2021, what would have been Siu-Ling's 58th birthday, approached, I decided it was time to pull myself together and get my book done as my birthday gift to her. A gift to honor the love between us, that special bond between parent and child that transcends all dimensions. A gift Siu-Ling would want me to share with you.

CHAPTER 1

An Unexpected Journey

We cannot change the cards we are dealt, just how we play the game.
~Randy Pausch

"I wanted to look after you in your old age. Instead, you are looking after me on my death bed," my daughter, Siu-Ling, said ruefully as I sat at her bedside. Those words seared my very soul, and in spite of the pain in my heart, I could not feel sorry for myself, because I did not want her to feel guilty about something none of us had any control over.

I tried to compose myself and gently reminded her of the day the ambulance took me to the hospital when she was three years old. She used to tell me how scared she had been, thinking I had died when I did not come home that day, nor for several days after. I told her that, although my heart had stopped beating that day, I did not die. "The doctors were able to save me. I came back so I could be here for you," I said as I lovingly stroked her arm, trying not to cry.

I remember the day that my heart stopped. It happened the day after we moved into our new house in a Montreal suburb in 1966. We had two little children; Siu-Ling was three and a half years old and her little brother, Jeff, two. I was in the third trimester of my pregnancy and looking forward to our third child, a little brother or sister for Siu-Ling and Jeff.

The morning after we moved in, our children were running around the house excitedly, exploring their new surroundings and playing hide and seek among the packing boxes. I was in the bathroom when I noticed an alarming symptom that indicated a medical emergency. My husband, Bing, phoned my obstetrician, who told him to keep me in bed. Several hours later, I started hemorrhaging. Alarmed, my husband phoned the doctor once again and was told to call an ambulance. Several neighbors came running to the house when the ambulance, with sirens blaring, rushed me to the hospital. Two of our new neighbors offered their teenage daughters to help my distraught husband and confused little children by babysitting Siu-Ling and Jeff if needed.

Upon arriving at the hospital, medical staff hooked me up to an IV and tried to stabilize me. My doctor was not there and, somehow, nobody seemed to know what to do. They thought I was about to give birth when my baby was not due for another two months.

By the time the doctor finally arrived, several hours later, I had lost so much blood that I went into shock. After examining me, he barked orders at medical staff to rush me into the operating room. Two nurses rolled the bed I was lying on into the dim hallway and started running, pushing the bed along, their footsteps clip-clopping on the shiny tile floor. In the meantime, the doctor called my husband before the emergency surgery to inform him of my grave condition and to ask him the unfathomable question, "Do you want me to save your wife ... or the baby?"

As soon as I was transferred into the OR and onto the operating table under bright overhead surgical lights, somebody put a mask on my face and told me to count backward from ten to one while a nurse with a big pair of scissors started cutting my clothes off my body. It did not take long for me to lose consciousness, at which point I unexpectedly found myself looking down from a corner of the ceiling at my own body on the operating table. It was as if I was leaning out a window from the waist up, watching the doctors and nurses hovering over my body below. Suddenly, a nurse in a white uniform and nurse's cap appeared beside the me on the ceiling. I don't know where she came from. Strangely enough, she was only there from the waist up as well. She explained what was happening below when I suddenly felt as if an unknown force whisked me out of the operating room into outer space. It was dark, but I saw specks of bright lights everywhere. I was floating around, feeling happy and as light as a feather. Suddenly, fireworks started exploding all around me just before I was sucked into a tunnel. I could hear the pounding of my heart like the clickety-clack of a train. At the far end of the tunnel, I saw a heavy door with bright, white, silvery light bursting from beneath it like a waterfall. When I was pulled deeper into the tunnel, I looked back at where I had come from and saw the light at the tunnel entrance getting smaller and smaller. That's when, to my subconscious horror, I realized I was dying. I wanted to scream but could not. "No, ... no!" I moaned. "I don't want to die. I can't die! I have two little children. They need me. I can't leave them." Suddenly it was as if the light went out, and I was engulfed in oblivion.

The following day, I found myself lying in a hospital room. Weak light filtered in through the window. My chest felt bruised and sore. I didn't know where I was or what had happened until I vaguely saw my husband sitting beside my bed, stroking my head. I was confused and trying to remember what had happened when my obstetrician walked in to check on me. Without saying hello or good morning, the first thing he said was, "You must have been a bad girl when you were little."

"Eh? What do you mean?" I asked weakly.

"Your heart stopped beating," he said matter-of-factly. "We had to resuscitate you."

His words did not make sense, and I didn't understand what he was saying. He then turned to my husband and started talking to him, but whatever he said went over my head. I kept wondering why he told me that I was a bad girl when I was little. Why? What did I do? What did he know?

I lost my baby, a little boy. I never saw him and never had a chance to hold him. I carried him close to my heart for seven months, and suddenly he was gone, leaving an emptiness in my being that bewildered me. What happened? Where was my baby?

The day I was rushed to hospital in an ambulance left an indelible imprint on my children, but especially on Siu-Ling, who understood that something was seriously wrong. She was only three and a half years old but very much aware of what was going on around her. She later told me, "Dad was crying. He was sitting on the chair in the living room, holding Jeff on one knee and me on the other. I thought you had died. We all cried." It broke my heart when I found out how that terrible time upset my little girl and still affected her many years after.

I survived, and life went on despite the hole in my heart that only I knew was there. My pain at losing my baby was made even worse because hospital staff put me in the maternity ward after I lost my baby. Was that the ill-conceived notion of how hospitals handled patients who had lost their babies in the 1960s? I shared a room with a woman who had just given birth to a baby boy. They brought him in to be nursed several times during the day, and later that night they wheeled in his little bassinette and placed it beside her bed. The side of my bed remained empty. My breasts were engorged, and I had no baby to feed.

While I was in the hospital, my husband went to the funeral home to arrange our baby's funeral. He took Siu-Ling and Jeff with him, because there was nobody to look after them. Siu-Ling told me about the day they visited the funeral home. She said she was scared and crawled under the big fancy desk in the funeral director's office, listening to her dad and the funeral director talk. She did not know about the baby and was sure they were discussing arrangements for my funeral. I can't imagine the anxiety my poor little girl must have been experiencing. That was an episode in her life she never forgot.

After two weeks in the hospital, I was finally able to get out of bed. When my husband came in for a visit, he told me to stand by the window overlooking the parking lot and wave, so our two toddlers waiting in the parking lot below could see me and be assured I was not dead. Imagine! In this day and age, there is no way anyone would leave two little kids alone in a parking lot.

After I came home from the hospital, friends awkwardly tried to comfort me by saying, "You can have another child." Sure! Just like having another piece of cake? "You're lucky you already have two!" another said. So? What was that supposed to mean? Can't we have more than two children? I came from a family of four, and so did my husband.

It is said that time heals all wounds. No! That is not true. Not this kind of wound. Yes, the pain will, perhaps, lessen over time, but such a wound never heals. It never goes away. It leaves a permanent scar. My baby was a part of me. When he died, I felt like part of my heart was torn away, leaving an emptiness only I knew about. If you don't know what to say to someone who just lost a child, please, try not to say anything. A silent, sympathetic hug or a quiet pat would be more meaningful than those well-worn platitudes people tend to say because they don't know what to say.

As I sat by Siu-Ling's side that day, more than 50 years had passed since I lost my baby. I never thought I would be sitting at my daughter's deathbed. What did I do to deserve the most heart-wrenching pain a parent could possibly endure once again? I felt emotionally numb. I was just sitting and watching my daughter's life ebb away, like watching the tide draining away from the shore, unable to do anything to stop it. She was my daughter, my love, my life, my pride, and my joy. This couldn't be happening! It's not fair! It is against the rules of nature for parents to outlive their child. Let's face it, death is an inevitable part of life that none of us can escape. And we don't get to choose when it comes. Death doesn't only pick the sick, old, and infirm but also takes the young, innocent, vibrant, and healthy among us.

My child was much too young and still had so much to give to make this world a better place. She led a healthy, active life, was kind, loving, and giving. Why did she have to get sick and die? Why? I would have given my life for her. What could I do to make her well again?

I imagined myself holding my hands over her body; I imagined healing energies flowing out of them that would annihilate her cancer and chase death away. I kept hoping for a miracle that did not come, until finally the cruel pain of reality scorched my aching heart. I sat at the foot of her bed as I massaged her legs, swollen with edema. Her skin felt cool and silky smooth from the lotion I had applied. I still had her. She was still with me, but in what condition and for how long? Watching my child wither away from an incurable disease was not something any parent ever imagines. The palliative care physician, who visited almost daily in Siu-Ling's final days, told us her heart was still strong, but she would die in only a matter of days because her kidneys had started shutting down. Siu-Ling remained lucid, her dignity still intact, but the thought that she could become delirious, experience alarming breathing changes, and lose control of her bodily functions before death took her in its grip was unthinkable. How could we let her go through that?

Hot tears streamed down my cheeks, although I tried to hold them back. If my tears could wash cancer away, I would let them flow profusely. When Siu-Ling saw me cry, she said, in no uncertain terms, in spite of her weakened condition, "Mom, I don't want you to cry." I had to get up and retreat to my room, where I hugged my pillow and poured my tears onto it. I groped for something, anything, to hang onto as I drowned in my sorrow. Why? Why my child? It should have been me. But each life has its own destiny, and like a river flowing to the sea, we cannot change its course. Rivers are living, moving parts of the earth. Sometimes they flow smoothly and gently gurgle along; at other times, they ripple and rush through rapids, only to crash with a thundering roar into the shallows below.

Our life on earth is limited by time and death. It is the nature of things. We are born, and we die. I had been given a second chance after my unexpected brush with death. Who decides when it's time for us to go? It was her time, not mine. Just as the sun goes up in the morning, it goes down when the day is done. My day was not done and Siu-Ling's was about to end.

CHAPTER 2

Looking Back in Time

Life is what happens when you're busy making other plans.
~ John Lennon

In 1958, my husband and I left our home and families in Indonesia and moved to Germany, where my husband had been offered an engineering position with Siemens & Halske, one of Germany's legendary electrical engineering companies.

Siu-Ling, our first child, was born in Munich on January 22, 1963. She was perfect, a healthy and robust baby with bright brown, almond-shaped eyes and rosy cheeks. As a baby, she already had the eyes of an observer and thinker. There was something earnest about her, but also a glint of glee in her sparkling eyes. I often wondered what went on in that little head of hers. It was a joy to see this tiny creature grow into a little girl with a personality and mind of her own.

We were about to move back to Indonesia a couple of months after Siu-Ling was born when our parents warned us not to come back because of the political and civil unrest brewing in Indonesia. It eventually led to what became known as an *Orgy of Violence*, one of the bloodiest mass murders of the 20th century. Between 500,000 and one million alleged communist party members and sympathizers were killed by the Indonesian army, paramilitary, and religious mobs all over the country. People disappeared in the middle of the night, never to be seen again. I remember hearing about rivers red with blood because the executioners dumped hundreds of corpses into rivers after they slaughtered them. The killings spread beyond suspected communists to target ethnic Chinese, university students, and union members.

During this time, my brother was a university student and an active member of the Indonesian Christian Student Association. When civil unrest became palpable on campus, a military guard always accompanied my brother to and from university for his safety as a Christian student activist of Chinese origin. On the only day his guard did not show up, a group of Islamic students he did not know grabbed him and took him to a command post in town, a Chinese school that the insurgents had confiscated from the local Chinese community. They dragged my brother into one of the rooms in this building, its shuttered windows keeping prying eyes from seeing what went on inside its dim and dank interior. But my brother saw the white-washed walls spattered with blood, showing it for the crime scene it was. They pushed him across a floor sticky with red and brown stains that turned out to be blood. Fear hung in the air, and the stench of blood and sweat was nauseating. They took him to that room to put fear into him and to show him what these revolutionaries were capable of if they did not like who he was or what he represented.

After taking my brother to the room, which they used for torturing their captives, his captors dragged him outside to face their leader and his henchmen. As they were going through the courtyard, he saw a crumpled, bloodied heap of a man sprawled on the basketball court. The man had been seriously beaten and tortured. It was hard to tell if he was alive or dead. At that moment, an approaching pick-up truck revved its engine and deliberately drove towards the body on the ground, aiming its wheels at the man's head. A sickening crack made my brother jump back with a start, gripped by nausea when he saw bone and brain matter spattered on the ground. The sound, sight, and smell of that horrifying incident still haunt him to this day. So, what happened after? How did he avoid a similar fate?

He was shaking with fear and felt sick to his stomach when he noticed a familiar-looking car driving into the schoolyard. Everybody's eyes turned to the car. Why did it come, and who was in it? That's when my brother recognized our father's driver, *Pak* Wongso (*Pak,* short for *Bapak,* is Indonesian, meaning "father" or "older man") at the wheel. How did he get here, and why had he come?

When the car stopped and the doors opened, my brother saw my father and another man step out of the vehicle. The man accompanying my father was a close family friend we called *Oom* (Dutch for "uncle"). He happened to be at our parents' home when word reached my father that a group of militant students had abducted my brother from the university. It was well known where they took their captives, and, together with his friend, our dad immediately went to the command post to find my brother. It so happened that our family friend, *Oom* Didi, was none other than Major General

Didi Kartasasmita, a well-known officer of the Indonesian National Armed Forces. He resolutely strode towards the men surrounding my brother and ordered them to release him, admonishing them in no uncertain terms. When my brother's captors recognized this high-ranking military commander, they immediately became submissive, bowing with hands in a prayer position, rocking back and forth as they apologized for their mistake and begged for forgiveness. If it had not been for *Oom* Didi, who knows what might have happened to my brother?

Those horrifying incidents marked the beginning of the Turbulent Sixties in Indonesia. They were the reason my parents warned us not to come back. We then decided to get together with several compatriots living, working, or studying in Munich to discuss our future. What should we do, and where should we go if we chose not to go back to Indonesia?

In Search of A Home

Sometimes you just know it's time to start something new and
trust the magic of beginnings.
~Meister Eckhart

After careful consideration, we decided that we could not stay in Germany, where locals still viewed Asians with suspicion. I remember old women at the bus stop, wearing sensible shoes and carrying shopping bags, eyeing me as one of them elbowed the other, jutting her chin in my direction and saying loud enough for me to hear, "*Schau! Ausländer!*" (Look! Foreigner!)

One of our Chinese-Indonesian friends in Munich had a daughter in elementary school, where children sang the German national anthem before class started. Of course, this little girl sang along with the rest of the class. Afterward, her classmates asked, "Why are you singing *our* national anthem? You are not German."

After many late nights discussing different options with our compatriots, we decided to move to Canada, hoping that Canada would accept us for who we were and what we could contribute to this country we chose to live in to secure a better life for ourselves, our children, and our futures.

Even though we knew very little about Canada, my image of it came from what I remembered from the movie *Rosemarie*. To me, Canada was a vast country with wild forests, lakes, snow-covered mountains, and handsome Mounties. I still remember Howard Keel singing a haunting Indian love song to proclaim his love for Rosemarie, a beautiful Indian maiden, as his voice echoed through the Rocky Mountains. That scene was so beautiful it sent shivers up my spine. That impression of Canada as love and nature had become etched in my mind. To me, Canada signified adventure and new beginnings.

We immigrated to Canada in November 1963 and landed in Montreal on a gloomy, drizzly day, the beginning of our new adventure. Siu-Ling was almost ten months old. She was such a good baby and did not fuss throughout the more than 10-hour flight from Munich, which included a stopover in Amsterdam. We were pleasantly surprised at the airport when Canada's customs officer bid us a warm welcome after going through our immigration papers. He even handed us a form and explained that we would be eligible for a Family Allowance for our baby. Family Allowance? We never heard of a Family Allowance before. What a welcome surprise to learn that, as new immigrants, we could claim this benefit toward the care, maintenance, education, or training of our child until she reached the age of eighteen.

Lee, one of our Chinese-Indonesian friends we first met in Munich, was married to a Bavarian woman. He had preceded us to Canada with his family, and they made Montreal their new home. It is interesting to note that most of my native German friends who immigrated to Canada in the 1960s were married to foreigners, as mixed marriages were still frowned upon in Germany at that time.

Lee welcomed us at the airport in Montreal and found us a place to stay for the night before he helped us find an apartment. We were young and had no trouble settling into this new country in the middle of a bleak winter, far away from our homeland and all that was familiar to us. Luckily, our friend Lee and my husband, both engineers, had no problems finding jobs.

As new immigrants, we had no family in Canada and had to fend for ourselves, but we knew Lee and his wife, Erika, who had a little girl, Daniella, the same age as Siu-Ling. My husband and I continued speaking German with Lee and Erika and our little girls.

Because Indonesia was a Dutch colony, my husband and I grew up speaking Dutch at home and with friends who had attended Dutch schools. We continued to converse in Dutch with each other when we wanted to have a private conversation in Siu-Ling's presence. During one such conversation, we were astounded when two-year-old Siu-Ling suddenly retorted in perfect Dutch: *Ik weet wel wat je zegt* (I know very well what you said). Siu-Ling's ability to observe and absorb at that tender age also defined her as an adult.

When Siu-Ling was 22 months old, a little brother, Jeff, was born. Right from the start, she was the big sister, the one in charge. For her third birthday, we bought her a shiny red tricycle. It didn't take her long to learn to ride it. One day she decided to take her little brother for a ride on the deck behind the seat while he hung onto her. They had a lot of fun as they zoomed back and forth on the sidewalk in front of our apartment.

Jeff was barely two years old when she wanted to know what would happen if he did not hang on to her when she started pedaling. Little brother did what big sister told him and let go as she stepped on the pedals. Whoa! The result was inevitable. When Siu-Ling started to pedal, Jeff was thrown off the tricycle, bawled his head off, and ended up with a bump on his head. How could I be angry when all she did was contemplate cause and effect, creating an experiment to find out what would happen if he let go when she started pedaling?

Siu-Ling on the tricycle with Jeff clinging to her.

Two years later, I was expecting our third child. After living in an apartment, it was time for our growing family to move into a house with a garden. We settled for Beaconsfield, just outside Montreal. It was a nice, friendly neighborhood where people reached out to us the day after we had moved into our new home — the day I was rushed to the hospital by ambulance.

CHAPTER 3

The Way We Were

One way to get the most out of life is to look upon it as an adventure.
~William Feather

Life in Beaconsfield was peaceful and quiet. Our neighbors were friendly, and we often stopped to chat with them when we were outside. We became good friends with the two neighbors who offered their daughters to babysit our children the day I was rushed to the hospital. We invited each other for tea or dinner from time to time. Norma and Scott, who lived across the street from us, even invited us to stay at their Vermont cottage. Our children played together, running and biking up and down our quiet neighborhood and going in and out of each others' homes and gardens. In winter, they built snow forts and had snowball fights. One day, Jeff and Johnny (another neighbor's son) spent hours creating a snow fort in our garden. When they came in from the cold for a cup of hot chocolate, Johnny told me Jeffrey had made a fart.

"So?!"

"That was rude," Johnny said.

"Rude? Why? There is plenty of snow out there. Jeff can make all the forts he wants."

Johnny looked at me with a gaping mouth. Soon word spread around our neighborhood that Jeff's mom did not know what a fart was. "Fart" and "fort" sounded the same to me. I did not know what a fart was. It was not a word I learned in school.

When we obtained our Canadian citizenship in 1968, it was one of the most important events of our lives. Canada was our home, and being part of this great country was worth celebrating. We had a party with our many Canadian friends who had moved to Canada from at least half a dozen different countries. I love Canada's multicultural tapestry of people from all over the world.

We lived next-door to a French-Canadian family who were being snubbed by the other neighbors in our predominantly Anglo community where most people were of British origin. *Two Solitudes,* a book by Hugh MacLennan published in 1945, revolves around the relationship between English and French-speaking Canadians. The phrase "Two Solitudes" later came to denote a perceived lack of communication and a lack of will to communicate between people of British and French ancestry in Canada.

As a person who was neither English nor French, I became aware of this subtle aloofness between my English and French-Canadian neighbors. Whenever I was outside chatting with a group of my English-speaking neighbors, they would wave but snicker when our French neighbor, Paule, drove by in her fancy sports car. "There she goes again," they'd say. *So what?* Paule was a neighbor, a friend, a lawyer, and a well-known French-Canadian author. Her husband, Jean Claude Delorme, also a lawyer, was Secretary and General Counsel for the Expo 67 world exhibition in Montreal to celebrate Canada's Centennial Year. He was later named Officer of the Order of Canada for his contribution to Expo 67.

Paule worked on a bilingual children's television series for the CBC (Canadian Broadcasting Corporation). One day she asked me if I would be interested in collaborating with her. Collaborating? I wasn't sure what she meant. She said she would write the French dialogue and asked if I would help write the English lines. I was pretty surprised, for I had never written a script for television, but it was an exciting challenge and an offer I could not refuse. What was interesting was that we had been casually chatting about children, children's stories, languages, and our backgrounds for a while. I was not aware that she had been quietly assessing me during those conversations before making that offer to work with her.

Paule and I became close friends. She kindled my interest in writing and, together, we wrote dozens of scripts for the bilingual CBC children's television series *Chez Hélène.* I had so much fun writing our stories and seeing them come alive on screen. The show, aimed at English-speaking preschoolers, was considered an unusual attempt to promote Canadian unity by exposing English-speaking children to the French language in a fun and playful manner.

The 15-minute morning show was about Hélène, a warm and friendly French-speaking grandmotherly lady who introduced the French language to countless English-speaking children who watched her show. She told French stories and taught French songs. Louise was a visiting English and French-speaking friend who switched between English and French as she repeated and translated Hélène's dialogue. Susie, the third character in the series, was a cute, English-speaking mouse puppet.

Paule lived behind us, and our doors were always open to each other. Whenever an inspiration struck either one of us, we would drop in on each other, regardless of the time, day or night, especially when we had a deadline to meet. We would sit, discuss, write, and ruminate over the script until the wee hours of the morning. Paule was the person who signed the contract with the CBC. I was only a collaborator working in the background. My name never appeared in the credits, but I did not think anything of it because I liked what I was doing and was happy to earn a little bit of money.

I worked on the television series with Paule for at least two years, until 1971, and enjoyed being involved in one of my children's favorite television programs. Whenever I got stuck, I would often ask Siu-Ling, "What do you think Susie would say?" or "What do you think Susie should do?" Susie, the mouse, was supposed to be a little preschooler, and Siu-Ling always knew what to say because she could put herself in Susie's shoes and relate things to me.

When Siu-Ling started kindergarten at the age of five, she already read chapter books like *The Adventures of Tom Sawyer and Huckleberry Finn* by Mark Twain. She loved books and was a prolific reader. A couple of weeks after she started grade one, her teachers decided that she should skip a grade because she was too advanced. I remember her telling me how a couple of her classmates followed her and their teacher down the hall, chattering excitedly as they accompanied Siu-Ling to the grade two class. Everybody helped carry her belongings to her new class. Nobody had ever skipped a grade before, and to her former classmates and the rest of the kids in school, Siu-Ling was a superstar. Luckily, it never went to her head. It was just something that happened, and that was it.

Siu-Ling loved school from day one and decided it was time for her three-year-old brother to learn to read because there was so much to learn and discover by reading. Teacher Siu-Ling was very strict and took her job quite seriously. Although Jeff preferred playing with his cars, Siu-Ling always managed to make him pay attention. She had everything in her teaching schedule. There were lessons to be learned, and there was a time for snacks and a time for play. Jeff looked up to his big sister, because she knew everything and always looked out for him.

At that time, Siu-Ling and Jeff were the only kids of Chinese descent in our neighborhood. When Jeff started kindergarten, a bunch of older kids teased him and made fun of him because of this. One day, they cornered him and started taunting him and pushing him around when suddenly, out of nowhere, big sister appeared and waded into the group of tormenters. She was visibly angry but, with determination and without losing her cool, she approached the one she identified as the ringleader. She gave him a stern mouthful as the rest of the gang slowly backed off, shocked at the fierceness of this little Chinese girl. That was the last time they ever bullied Jeff. It was one reason Jeff considered his big sister a hero.

A Musical Journey

Music gives a soul to the universe, wings to the mind, flight to the imagination, and life to everything.
~Plato

One day, Paule told me about Madame Lecomte, a music teacher in our neighborhood. Paule asked if I would be interested in enrolling Siu-Ling in music lessons. Of course! Music was part of my childhood. My mother played the piano. I did too. My mind wandered off to Mister Lopez, my old piano teacher who came to the house for my private lessons. He was a tall, skinny gentleman who smelled like mothballs. Mister Lopez reminded me of a vulture with his pale, dark skin, beaked nose, and greased greying hair combed straight back over his head. He always wore a long-sleeved white shirt with a bow tie. Standing beside me, hunched forward with his eyes half-closed while he listened to me play, he always had one arm folded over his stomach and one hand over his mouth as he stroked his upper lip with his thumb and forefinger.

Oh! Yes, Madame Lecomte... what about Madame Lecomte? Paule said Madame Lecomte was a highly respected music teacher. She thought Siu-Ling would enjoy taking music lessons from her. That's what I liked about Paule. She was such an inspiration, a visionary and humanitarian devoted to arts and culture. Her main interest was in children's education and the professional development of youth, while her husband, Jean-Claude, was a patron of the arts. He presided over the boards of *Les Grands Ballets Canadiens*, *Place des Arts*, and *l'Opéra de Montréal* at its creation. He was also one of the founding members of the National Gallery of Canada in Ottawa. Music and Art defined this fascinating couple who became two of my dearest friends. They stimulated my interest and love for music and art, often inviting me to a special concert or art exhibition.

I decided to enroll Siu-Ling in recorder lessons. That was the first musical instrument she learned to play. At the end of the year, Madame Lecomte organized a concert attended by the parents of her students. Siu-Ling was to play Johann Sebastian Bach's Minuet in G-minor, and I was to accompany her on the piano. We practiced together every day and had a lot of fun, pretending to be superstars.

On the day of the concert, Siu-Ling was calm and confident. After our recital, the parents in the audience gasped, got up, and, to my surprise, gave her an enthusiastic standing ovation. I held my breath and wasn't sure what to do. Then I saw little Siu-Ling face the crowd and bow her head, her recorder pressed against her chest, like a celebrated musician. I quickly got up, grabbed her by the hand, and took her to our seats in the audience amid more applause. Phew! Me being me, I felt a bit awkward amid that show of appreciation. I felt a bit uncomfortable, but that day started Siu-Ling on her musical journey. She played the recorder, even at that very first concert, with great feeling. Madame Lecomte told me that Siu-Ling had an ear for music. She recognized notes by ear, a rarity in such a young child. If I heard someone blow a note on the recorder, whether it was a C, D, E, F, or F-sharp, I could not tell the difference, but, amazingly, Siu-Ling could identify each note.

When Siu-Ling was eight years old and Jeff was six, we were blessed with a new addition, a long-awaited little brother we named Timothy. Holding this tiny baby in my arms, close to my heart, was the balm that soothed the rough edges of my ragged heart after losing my baby almost five years earlier. Timothy's birth marked a new chapter in our lives.

When I arrived home from the hospital with our new baby, I stood by our living room window, anxiously watching for Siu-Ling and Jeff to come home from school. Siu-Ling knew this was the day they would meet their long-awaited baby brother. It's strange, but I somehow remember the clothes she wore that day, yellow and white checkered seersucker gingham shorts and a matching sleeveless top with white zigzag trim on its ruffled bottom. I was holding and rocking the baby in my arms when I glimpsed something yellow in the distance, hopping down the street. I opened the door and went outside to see Siu-Ling and Jeff running to meet us, their rosy cheeks glowing and their eyes intently on the bundle in my arms.

"Our baby!" she squealed. "He's so tiny."

"Yes, he is …"

Siu-Ling was bursting with excitement as she touched and sniffed the baby's tiny hand, while Jeff was a bit restrained, unsure of what to make of this new little person everybody was so excited about. It was time for Siu-Ling and Jeff to get to know their new little brother.

Family

Although we had made many good friends, our family only consisted of my husband Bing, me, and our three little children. We lived in a country where we were transplanted and had no history and no roots. Our parents, grandparents, and siblings lived far, far away, on the other side of the world, where day to them was night to us and the other way around. It was therefore important to me that, in our little family, we were there for each other. We had to grow together and be strong as we established ourselves in this country.

It made me think of an old Chinese tale about the meaning of family. It was about a wise old woodcutter and his three sons, who were constantly bickering and gave him no peace. They all did their own thing and did not seem to care much about each other. One day, the old man decided to teach his children the importance of family and what it means to be part of a family. He handed each of his sons a single stick and asked them to break it in two. The boys had no trouble doing that. He then gave them each a bunch of sticks tied together. "Now, break this," he said. Not one was able to break the bunch of sticks, no matter how hard they tried. "This bunch of sticks," he said, "is like family. When you stick together and are there for each other, nobody will be able to break you. And that, my sons, is what family is about."

A New Adventure

In Canada, October 1970 became known as the October Crisis, which started with the kidnapping of James Cross, the British trade commissioner in Montreal. Cross was kidnapped by members of what was known as the *Front de Libération du Quebec* (FLQ), a militant part of the Quebec Sovereignty movement that advocated independence for the province of Quebec. It was a time of political unrest in an otherwise peaceful country. The kidnapping and murder of Pierre Laporte, Minister of Immigration and Labour, shortly after Cross was kidnapped, was the most serious terrorist act ever committed in Canada. It was also the first time in Canadian history when the War Measures Act, which deprived Canadian citizens of rights and freedom during peacetime, was invoked

Because of this crisis, my husband decided we should move out of Quebec. There was growing unease among the businesses and people living there because the threat that the province might secede from Canada hung over our heads. As a result of all this, the company my husband worked for started laying off its employees and then closed. Luckily, my husband had found an engineering job in Ottawa, Ontario, before the layoffs started.

Ottawa is a two-hour drive from Montreal, and for most of that first year, when Timothy was a baby, my husband commuted between Montreal and Ottawa, coming home every weekend. When Timmy was one year old, we decided to put our house up for sale and move to Ottawa.

I was sad to leave Montreal and the many good friends we had made in the nine years we lived in *la belle province*. Montreal was where we first set foot in Canada. We made it into our home, far away from the land where we were born. Canada is where we started a new life and made lifelong friends, one of whom, of course, was Paule. I was sorry that I could not continue working with her, but that did not mean the end of our friendship. Life goes on and, with three young children, we started a new chapter in our lives in Ottawa.

I was busy, but I made sure I was always home when the children came home from school and burst into the house looking for me. During the day, I volunteered at schools, the local hospital, and our small public library, which, at the time, was in a trailer. I also volunteered for the sports organizations our children were members of. They played soccer in summer and hockey in winter. We also started cross-country skiing as a family. The children later joined competitive cross-country ski teams in high school and college.

Winters in Canada are long. Rather than staying cooped up indoors to avoid the cold, we encouraged our children to play outdoors, learn how to skate, play hockey, go skiing, and make the most of winter. Winter became a season our children always looked forward to. Sitting by a cozy fire with a mug of hot cocoa after a ski outing is a fond remembrance.

The years passed quickly, and when Tim started grade one, I decided to go back to school. I was accepted into Carleton University's Master's program in German literature, where I was lucky to meet Professor Jutta Goheen. She inspired and encouraged me to focus on medieval German literature. This subject fascinated the old romantic in me, as pictures of brave and noble knights in shining armor, beautiful princesses with golden tresses, and castles on hilltops appeared in my mind. I became Professor Goheen's research assistant and received a graduate scholarship two years in a row. When I graduated in 1984, no one was prouder of me than Siu-Ling, who had started her undergraduate studies in biology at the University of Waterloo. Why biology? Siu-Ling loved nature and wanted to learn how all living and nonliving organisms interacted with each other. Since biology encompasses many different fields of research related to the sustainability of life, she could also learn about other subjects that interested her: the environment, ecosystems, and causes of illnesses, which, somehow, helped shape the world.

As a co-op student, which combines courses and field work, Siu-Ling conducted underwater experiments and sample collection by scuba diving. She was involved in researching the impact of acid rain on the Canadian Shield lakes. Her field experiences as an undergraduate student also included studying the feeding ecology of coyotes in Long Point, Ontario, and working as a field technician for projects on Arctic Char ecology in Ungava Bay, Northern Quebec. She told me about the day she was walking to camp from fieldwork when a couple of Inuit hunters she was approaching told her to keep walking, not to run, and not to look back. She was not aware that a young bear was following her. As soon as she was safely back at the camp, the hunters shot and killed the bear. I remember her telling me how sad she was for the bear, but such is life. Bear meat is considered a staple for Inuit, while bear fat is used as cooking oil or fuel for lamps. Bear skins are used for clothing and boots to keep them warm. Hunting is part of the Inuit way of being in ecological and spiritual harmony with their environment. That sparked Siu-Ling's interest in the Arctic, its way of life, and its environment.

The first time Siu-Ling came home from university for the holidays, brother Tim, who was nine or ten years old at the time, had gone to the flower shop in the nearby shopping mall to buy a rose with his own pocket money to welcome his sister home. It warmed my heart to see how much he loved and adored his big sister.

After Siu-Ling graduated with a Master of Science in Biology with a specialization in freshwater ecology in 1988, she took a year off. Together, she and I traveled through Europe and went backpacking in Greece. We flew to Athens and took the ferry to the Island of Hydra, a small, picturesque island with amazing views of the surrounding Aegean Sea. We stayed at a bed and breakfast, which coincidentally was run by a couple who used to own a restaurant in the town of Waterloo, in Ontario, near the university Siu-Ling attended. Hydra is a small island, and there wasn't much to do there. Wandering around its hilly streets with centuries-old buildings and monasteries took us back in time. We explored the island on foot. By law, cars and motorcycles are not allowed. The only motorized vehicles on the island are garbage trucks. Horses, mules, donkeys, and water taxis provide public transportation. Otherwise, people either walk or bike to wherever they want to go.

One day, while eating dinner at an outdoor restaurant, the chef treated us to a glass of ouzo after dinner. I took one sip and almost choked because of its high alcohol content. This anise-flavored liqueur is Greece's national drink. I did not want to insult our host, so at his urging, Siu-Ling and I had another sip, and then another. I enjoyed the nice, sweet taste, until I felt my face getting hot and my head spinning. I only had three sips, but it was enough to make me burst into uncontrollable giggles. I could not help myself and must have embarrassed my daughter, who looked at me with an indulgent grin as she shook her head and rolled her eyes up when she ushered me out amid the chuckles of the patrons in the restaurant.

Backpacking with my daughter was quite an adventure. It was during these outings that she took over and became my guide. I had complete trust in her and always felt perfectly safe with Siu-Ling by my side. She always knew where we were going, what to see, and what to do. Those moments always filled my heart with love and gratitude -- my daughter and I in the great wide world, creating memories to treasure. We went to Greece and later to Holland, where we popped into the gloomy interior of a coffee shop in Amsterdam to have a cup of coffee and apple pie. We did not realize that in Amsterdam, a "coffee shop" was an establishment selling pot. No wonder it smelled funny in there. Wherever we wandered, in Germany, France, England,

Indonesia, China, Malaysia, or Australia, Siu-Ling was my guide and the person I depended on. Our roles of mother and daughter reversed, and she took care of me. Not just when we were traveling together, but in life, in general.

Siu-Ling's first job after she graduated from university was as an Environmental Analyst for a corporation in Ottawa. During that time, she did some field work in Nunavut, which rekindled her interest in the Arctic. That led to a job as an Ecologist for the

Siu-Ling and me on a hike in Auyuituk Park on Baffin Island.

Department of Indian and Northern Affairs, where she worked with a group of environmental scientists charged with looking at the quality of the Arctic environment. The program she worked in, the Northern Contaminants Program (NCP), coordinates Canada's actions on contaminants, including Persistent Organic Pollutants (POPs) and mercury, both nationally and internationally. It was established in 1991 through Canada's Green Plan. As part of NCP's management team, Siu-Ling specialized in assessing how exposure to POPs impacted Inuit health. She drafted international protocols for POPs and was also part of a team that developed a strong liaison with Inuit leaders to develop effective dietary advice for Inuit that would be compatible with their traditional lifestyle. Siu-Ling quickly earned the respect of scientists and Inuit hunters alike. When asked her secret for forging such strong working relationships, she simply replied: Be kind.

After she completed that work, her interest in the Arctic intensified as she made more research and field trips to sites in Nunavut in Canada's Eastern Arctic, the Agassiz Ice Cap on Ellesmere Island, and Prince Leopold Island, where she worked as Camp Manager and Project Assistant, observing seabird colonies for a National Geographic film, *Life on the Edge*.

In the meantime, she studied Inuktitut, the native language of Nunavut, completing Nunavut's Arctic College 3-week intensive introductory and intermediate courses. She learned advanced Inuktitut at the Pirurvik Centre, an Inuit language school in Iqaluit. She also had a private tutor. Being able to read Inuit syllabics and converse in Inuktitut gave Siu-Ling the ability to communicate with and learn from Inuit elders. It was important

Siu-Ling and her team on one of her field trips.

to her to integrate Inuit Traditional Knowledge, known as Inuit Qaujimajatuqangik (IQ) and "western science" in Nunavut's wildlife research and management programs.

In 1998, when a job came up in the Department of Sustainable Development, Siu-Ling moved to Nunavut to start working as Manager of Wildlife Research for the Government of Nunavut. In 2004, she began work as a Habitat Biologist in the Environmental Conservation Branch of the Canadian Wildlife Service (CWS) of Environment Canada. One year later, Siu-Ling was promoted to Head of the Eastern Arctic Unit of CWS.

CHAPTER 4

The Moment Everything Changed

Challenges are what make life interesting.
Overcoming them is what makes life meaningful.
~Joshua J. Marine

In 2003, the Ontario Government designated SARS (severe acute respiratory syndrome) as a reportable, contagious, and virulent disease under the Health Protection and Promotion Act. On March 26, 2003, then Ontario Premier Ernie Eves declared SARS a provincial emergency. Hospitals were required to limit visitors and, by the end of the month, officials implemented access restrictions in all hospitals in Ontario.

2003 was also the year when Siu-Ling came home to Ottawa from Iqaluit for a medical appointment. She told me about getting a massage from a massage therapist who was visiting Iqaluit. When she laid herself down on her stomach, she felt as if there was a lump on the surface of the massage table. Upon closer inspection, however, there was nothing there. The protuberance she felt was in her stomach. She immediately went to the doctor to have it checked. The doctor wanted her to see a gynecologist. Unfortunately, there were no specialists in Iqaluit. The doctor suggested that Siu-Ling wait for a visiting gynecologist to come to Iqaluit in another two or three weeks. There was no way she would wait that long. She knew how serious this might be and asked her doctor to make an appointment with a specialist in Ottawa as soon as possible.

She flew to Ottawa, where she had an appointment with a specialist at Ottawa General Hospital on April 7. I came with her. When we arrived at the hospital, I discovered that the specialist she had the appointment with was at the cancer center. Cancer center? Why the cancer center? I started feeling uneasy, but Siu-Ling told me not to worry. "There's no point in worrying," she said, "if you don't know what to worry about." Of course, she was right. Still, I couldn't help feeling apprehensive.

I was in the waiting room when she came out after seeing the doctor. I sensed something was amiss, even though she did not let on there was anything seriously wrong. She was businesslike and told me that she was going to have exploratory surgery the following week.

Her surgery was scheduled for April 14. When her dad, brother Jeff, and I took her to the hospital, we learned that only patients were allowed in. Security staff at the entrance turned us away due to SARS restrictions. We anxiously said goodbye and wished her good luck. Before she went in, she turned around, gave me a tight hug and, with that typical Siu-Ling smile, she told us not to worry. Everything would be alright. With heavy hearts, we let her go, drove home, and waited for a call from the hospital, hoping and praying all would be well.

I was puttering around the house, trying to keep myself busy, when the shrill sound of the phone pierced the stillness in our home. I jumped up and, with shaking hands, picked up the phone. It was the surgeon. In a calm voice, he said they had operated on Siu-Ling, and without dilly-dallying, he told me, "It is cancer!" My heart sank, and my knees gave out as I clutched the phone and started hyperventilating before dropping to the floor, hugging my knees in despair.

"How is she?" I moaned, barely able to breathe.

"She is still sedated."

"When ... are you going to tell her?"

"Tomorrow morning."

"Can I at least be with her when you tell her?"

"No! Nobody is allowed in the hospital because of SARS."

Grabbing for words, I told him how horrible it would be for her to be alone when he told her the bad news. The surgeon took pity on me when I started crying. "Okay," he said, "be here tomorrow morning at 7:00. That's when I do my rounds. If security won't let you in, tell them you have an appointment with me. Have them page me, and I'll come and get you." My heart was shattered, but I was grateful for this small mercy.

After a sleepless night, my husband, our son Jeff, and I drove to the hospital under an early morning overcast sky that weighed heavily on us. Rush hour had started, and traffic slowed down to a crawl as we headed east from the western outskirts of Ottawa. My husband drove, and I sat beside him, lost in a daze. Neither of us said anything. It was as if the anguish we felt had muzzled us as we tried to grasp the gravity of that horrible diagnosis. Jeff knew how frightening a cancer diagnosis was. He was stunned and could not believe that cancer could strike his strong and healthy sister, but, like his sister and his dad, he was pragmatic. He later told me that he decided to support Siu-Ling any way he could and, without sounding glum, he intended to make the most of every moment they shared. Upon arrival at the hospital, security barred us from entering the premises. When I told the guard that we had an appointment with the doctor, he looked at me as if he thought, "Yeah, I've heard that before." I told him to page the doctor, and he reluctantly did.

A couple of minutes later, the doctor came down to greet us. "Come in," he said, looking at me. When the three of us stepped forward, he held up his hand to stop us. He then put up one finger and said, "Only one." I stepped forward, for if only one of us could go in, it should be me, Siu-Ling's mother. Disappointed, my poor husband and son had to wait outside, feeling helpless and lost.

As the doctor guided me onto the escalator to the second floor, I asked about my daughter's operation. He explained that it was ovarian cancer and that he had removed her ovaries and uterus.

"That means she'll never be able to have children," I remarked sadly.

"Your daughter's health is more important than for her to have children," he replied. He then pointed out her room and said he'd come by later.

I quietly entered the room. Siu-Ling was still half asleep and surprised to see me.

"Why are you here?" she asked. "I thought nobody was allowed in the hospital."

I tried to dodge her question and mumbled, "I know."

My daughter knew me well enough to suspect there was more to tell. After a moment, she asked if I knew anything. I did not want to lie and instead evaded the question by saying that this was why they let me come. She was quiet, and I could imagine the little wheels in her head turning. I held her hand and told her that whatever the outcome, I was there with her.

Shortly after, the doctor appeared, followed by a group of what I assumed were residents, medical students, and a nurse. As he waltzed into the room with his entourage, the first thing he said was, "Good morning! We operated on you yesterday ..." and then added without flinching, "It's cancer!" Just like that! It was almost as if he was saying, "It's raining." I was taken aback by the doctor's brashness, but if Siu-Ling was shocked or scared, she did not show it. I still had her hand in mine. She didn't say anything. She didn't blink. She did not even budge. After a couple of seconds, she said in a business-like manner, "Okay! So! What are *you* going to do about it?" I was stunned and, judging by the looks on their faces, so were the doctor and his crew.

In May, one month after her surgery, Siu-Ling started chemotherapy. Before she knew she had cancer, she had booked a flight to London to visit brother Tim in June. She had been looking forward to this trip, and there was no way she would cancel it. She intended to carry on, take control, live her life as best as she possibly could, and not let cancer rule her.

When she started losing her hair after chemo, she did not wait until her hair fell out in clumps. I accompanied her to the hairdresser when she decided to have her head shaved so she did not have to deal with losing her hair. She tried on a couple of wigs for fun and bought herself a nice one, but, in the end, she never used it. She preferred wearing hats, caps, or fancy scarves to cover her bald head.

While she carried on without ever complaining, I had to deal with the sorrow and fear of a disease that had hit Siu-Ling like a thunderbolt out of a clear blue sky. Why my child? I asked myself. Yes, why? She did not drink or smoke and never was sick in her life. She was physically active and spent a lot of time outdoors, hiking, biking, swimming, canoeing, and playing soccer in summer. In winter, she played hockey and went downhill and cross-country skiing. What did she do to deserve such a devastating diagnosis?

I, in the meantime, mourned the fact that my precious daughter had this damned disease that, for some unknown reason, picked her. Regardless of how she embraced life, it was heart-wrenching for me to have my daughter go through chemotherapy and lose her beautiful hair. I often cried myself to sleep, wondering why my daughter was cursed with such an affliction. Siu-Ling was young and healthy. The only time I remembered her getting sick, aside from the occasional cold, was when she had chicken pox when she was in kindergarten. Why did she have to have cancer? Why? It was not fair!

I know she would not want me to worry and think of a worst-case scenario. But, as a librarian, I could not help searching the Internet for information about ovarian cancer. According to the National Center for Biotechnology Information (NCBI), ovarian cancer is the most lethal gynecologic malignancy! It takes the lives of more than 15,000 women in the United States each year. J.A. Brucks of Brigham and Women's Hospital, Boston, Massachusetts, wrote that the overall 5-year survival rate for epithelial ovarian cancer remains approximately 30% and has not improved over the last three decades. Ovarian cancer is considered the fifth leading cause of cancer-related deaths in women. The survival rates for ovarian cancer are lower than for any other cancer that affects women.

What now? Fear gripped my heart as I tried to face my daughter's dire diagnosis. I didn't know what to do. Get on my knees and pray? Although I was brought up a Christian and attended Christian schools, I am not religious. I didn't know how to pray. I had recited the Lord's Prayer every night before I went to sleep for as long as I could remember, but it was a routine that didn't mean much to me. How could I suddenly beseech the Lord to make my daughter's cancer go away while I was lying in bed, staring into the dark night, desperate for a glimpse of light and a miracle?

In the meantime, friends and family in Canada, Holland, Indonesia, and Australia conducted prayer meetings for Siu-Ling in their churches. While I appreciated their devotion and trust in a higher being, I wondered if God would hear their prayers.

It made me think of another story from my childhood about the big flood when torrential rains soaked the land, drowning rice fields and people's livelihoods. People started praying for the rain to stop, but the rain kept pouring down from heaven above with no end in sight. They prayed and prayed some more. They chanted and danced to the beat of drums drowned out by rain and thunder. They begged the gods to please make it stop raining.

Finally, one of the farmers decided to visit the hermit who lived in a cave on top of the mountain. He was a wise old man who saw what was happening to the land and people below. The farmer told the hermit how they had prayed and offered gifts to the Rain God to stop the rain but to no avail. Sitting cross-legged as he stared into the distance, the hermit stroked his long white beard and calmly told the farmer, "Everybody prays for the gods to help them when they should first try to help themselves."

"How? How are we supposed to help ourselves?" the farmer implored.

"When your scythe is dull, what do you do?" the hermit asked.

"Well, sharpen it ... what does that have to do with all this rain?"

The old man nodded and continued, "When you have harvested your crop, what do you do?"

"Well, ... pack it and take it to market."

"That's right! The Gods won't sharpen your scythe or take your crop to market. Now think of what you could do with all this rain. Think of times when there is no rain, when the land is parched, and a drought destroys your crops."

It made the man think long and hard, and that's how terraced rice fields, canals, irrigation systems, and dams ended up being built.

While people can make some things happen, there was nothing I could do for my daughter. I could not climb a mountain to find a wise man or come closer to God and beg him to make my daughter's cancer go away. I could not blow, sweep, or wash it away. I felt utterly helpless. I know some people deeply believe in prayer. If it gives them comfort and makes them think that all will be well, that is wonderful. But all *I* could do was cry my eyes out in solitude. I did not want anyone to know the heartache I, as a mother, felt. I did not want Siu-Ling to see me cry, and I did not want to be a burden to my friends and family.

Was all this pain and anxiety what scientists refer to as anticipatory grief? Lynne Eldridge, MD, a lung cancer physician, describes anticipatory grief as "grief that occurs before death (or another great loss) in contrast to grief after death (conventional grief)." Eldridge explains that, rather than feeling grief for death alone, this type of grief also mourns, among other things, "the loss of dreams of what could be." That was certainly part of the pain I felt, knowing all that Siu-Ling would not experience if she died so young. She was in the middle of her life and at the height of her career, doing an important and meaningful job she was passionate about.

Siu-Ling must have spent a lot of time thinking and philosophizing about life and the impending losses of loved ones. She had friends who died young, and knowing that ovarian cancer is one of the deadliest cancers, she must have been pondering her own mortality. I happened to find these words of wisdom in one of Siu-Ling's journals. Her words made me think about the meaningful moments in life we like to remember. Nobody knows from one day to another what tomorrow might bring. Holding on to those precious moments gives us comfort when we need it.

I spend my days pursued by the shadows cast by losses yet to come and yet, knowing what one day will come to pass, despite our ignorance of when and how, we do little to prepare our souls for the loss of those we love. We may live in fear of those journeys not yet begun, but do we ensure the full reality of the present?

Do we sow the fields of the living with memories that can be harnessed and preserved to sustain us through the turbulent times when loss is most acute and irrevocable?

Do we envision the source of a future regret and mine it in the present? What will we need to keep us afloat in the affirmation of our personal tragedies?

Memories of laughter, of love, simply of time in one another's company.

(October 27, 2010)

Indeed! Why should I live in the shadow of a loss that may or may not happen in the foreseeable future? Shedding tears was *my way* of releasing the scorching pain in my chest and the pent-up emotions of the anxiety, sadness, and fear of losing my precious daughter. Crying is said to have a self-soothing effect. It activates the parasympathetic nervous system (PNS), which helps people relax. It also releases oxytocin and endorphins, two "feel good" hormones that can help lift people's spirits and make them feel better. So, let the tears flow and wash at least some of your pain away.

Dr. Judith Orloff, a psychiatrist on the UCLA Psychiatric Clinical Faculty, writes about the healing power of tears. "Tears are your body's release valve for stress, sadness, grief, anxiety, and frustration … after crying, our breathing and heart rate decrease, and we enter into a calmer biological and emotional state." We would be wise to heed Siu-Ling's words. Let's create and harness memories of laughter, love, and togetherness and preserve them to sustain us through turbulent times when the pain of irrevocable loss is most acute.

The Scourge of Cancer

Despite advances in modern medicine, according to the World Health Organization (WHO), cancer is still a leading cause of death worldwide. Although mortality rates have declined, the number of new cancer cases has increased.

In his book, *The Wisdom of the Wilderness*, Gerald May, a psychiatrist and theologian undergoing chemotherapy for lymphoma, wrote about his fellow patients in the cancer ward who spoke of *fighting* their cancers. In obituaries, one often reads about the deceased *battling* cancer or dying after a valiant *fight* with cancer. People talk about cancer as an enemy to be defeated. May said that his experience of the wilderness and nature made such "warlike references" feel wrong.

When I think about wilderness and nature, it reminds me of going for a walk in the forest on a beautiful autumn day. It is liberating to breathe in the smells of nature after a savage storm has blown leaves off trees and covered the ground with a blanket of leaves in all shapes, sizes, conditions, and colors. Life remains under that colorful carpet as it rustles, crackles, and crunches under our boots; a maple tree's crimson leaves stand out among the burnished brown, brass, copper, golden yellow, or speckled green of trembling aspen, poplars, cottonwood, and white birch leaves. While some leaves are still shiny and smooth, others are imperfect, misshapen, withered, tattered, and ravaged by the heat of the sun, insects, wind, and rain. All are products of nature.

Cancer is an aberration of nature, a proliferation of cells growing out of control. As Gerald May put it, "Like all other things in true nature, they (cancer cells) simply are what they are." As a biologist, Siu-Ling also perceived cancer as an aberration of nature. When she was first diagnosed with cancer, I asked, "Why you?" Her reply was, "Why not? According to cancer statistics, one in two people will develop cancer in their lifetime. In our family, it may as well be me. I am the only one who can best deal with it. It is what it is, and I do not want to burden my life with the forethought of dying. Having cancer does not mean I have to stop living." And so, she continued to live life to the fullest, doing things she always wanted to do with friends and family and spending time in nature and with her dogs.

In 1998, Siu-Ling first met Debbie McAllister in Revelstoke, BC, where she went backcountry skiing. Revelstoke is located in Canada's Rocky Mountains, 641 kilometers (398 mi) east of Vancouver. Debbie and Siu-Ling, along with a group of friends, flew by helicopter to Blanket Glacier, one of the best back-country skiing areas in the world. It marked the beginning of a deep, meaningful, and lifelong friendship. After that, Siu-Ling traveled to Revelstoke every winter to go skiing, even after her cancer diagnosis.

Siu-Ling loved the outdoors, animals, wilderness camping, canoeing, hiking, biking, telemarking, cross-country skiing, and skating. When she was ten years old, she started horseback riding, which became a passion. She later volunteered in a therapeutic horseback riding program for the disabled. During her school and university years, she participated in hockey, basketball, and triathlons.

Siu-Ling at the Blanket Glacier.

She embraced dog sledding after she moved to Baffin Island in 1998 to work for the territorial government of the Northwest Territories. This was shortly before its eastern part became Canada's newest territory, Nunavut, on April 1, 1999. Siu-Ling loved traveling, visiting Europe and Asia for work, as well as for pleasure, and Australia to visit family.

Siu-Ling was a voracious reader with an eclectic taste in books. She also loved to scribble and sketch, doodle, and draw. If she wasn't reading, she would be journaling, drawing, or softly singing while playing the guitar or piano during quiet times. I found journals and sketchbooks with her observations and descriptions of people, places, and things. I discovered she wrote poems, short stories, and an amazing array of words whose wisdom truly baffled me. Here is an example of one of Siu-Ling's sayings that I should take to heart: *If you spend all your time in the present worrying about sadness, pain, and tribulations you may experience in the future, you rob both the present and the future of any joy they may bring.*

CHAPTER 5

Life Goes On

Not how long but how well you have lived is the main thing.
~Seneca

After Siu-Ling completed her cancer treatment in November 2003, she flew back to her home in Iqaluit, went back to work, and resumed her life, taking care of her dogs, going dogsledding, and spending time with her friends and colleagues.

In April 2004, one year after her cancer diagnosis, with her cancer in remission, she felt well enough to join Matty McNair as one of the leaders on a dogsledding expedition to the Grinnell Glacier on Baffin Island with a group of British teenagers. Matty McNair, an American explorer living in Canada's Arctic, organized the trip for a British Broadcasting Corporation (BBC) reality television show called *Serious Arctic*. Matty, an adventurer and educator, is known internationally as one of the top polar guides in the world. She was a close friend of Siu-Ling's, and they had taken many dogsledding trips together on

Baffin Island over the years. Along with Paul Crowley, another Arctic adventurer, traveler, and good friend of Siu-Ling's, the three leaders guided the students, who were conducting research on global warming.

In the meantime, I continued working as a volunteer in a clinic at a local hospital, where I got to know the doctors and nurses in my department. We often had coffee together and chatted about our kids and families, exchanged recipes, talked about trips and the ups and downs of home, work, and life. I loved volunteering and helping where help was needed. It was a pleasant working relationship until I mentioned my apprehension about a recurrence of my daughter's cancer after a ten-year remission. Should I not have said anything? After working with these ladies for more than a decade, I thought it was something I could share with them. But instead, I noticed two of the nurses distancing themselves from me. At first, I did not think anything of it and thought it was just a passing phase which I did not attribute to what I had told them about my daughter's cancer.

When I came back from a holiday, I went up to one of these nurses to give her a hug like we usually did after one of us had been away, but when I approached her with open arms, she stepped back and put her hand up to stop me. I was shocked and didn't know what to make of it. It felt like my heart dropped to my feet. What happened? Why this sudden rebuff? Did I do something wrong? Was there something about me that scared her? Or … was it because I had told her that my daughter had cancer? Being snubbed like that made me feel like an outcast.

Was she afraid that the curse of cancer would rub off on her or her daughter? As a nurse, surely, she knew better. After years of supporting these women in their work and being there every week, it was a bitter pill to swallow. The other nurses in the department who saw this deplorable act felt terrible for me. They sympathized with me but did not dare say anything as they only worked there part-time and were afraid to get involved.

It especially hurt because I used to have amicable conversations with that nurse. Working in that clinic had been a pleasure until then, but the frostiness that descended on that department from that day on made me feel sick to my stomach. It's strange how some people react when they find out that someone they know has cancer. I no longer volunteer in that department, and, in spite of the pain that woman caused me, I must forgive her. Who knows what made her act that way?

My Inspiration

In 2007, four years after Siu-Ling's cancer diagnosis, I started taking an online creative writing course at the Institute for Children's Literature (ICL) to keep myself busy. It was a one-on-one, self-guided course. For my last assignment, I had the choice of either writing a fiction or nonfiction story. I chose non-fiction, because I love the excitement of research.

Siu-Ling with puppies Toko & Rohde and their mother Lao. (Photo credit: Elise Maltinsky)

After visiting Siu-Ling in Iqaluit and meeting her team of Inuit Dogs and her dog sledding friends, Siu-Ling encouraged me to write a book about the Inuit Dog. Inuit would not have survived life in one of the harshest environments on earth without their dogs, and in 1990, the Legislative Assembly of Nunavut selected the Canadian Inuit Dog (*canis familiaris borealis*) as the official animal of Nunavut. Based on archaeological evidence, the Canadian Inuit Dog, or *qimmiq* in Inuktitut, has been a resident of the Arctic for more than 4,000 years.

Since true Inuit Dogs are rarely seen south of the Arctic, I thought it was time to introduce the Canadian Inuit Dog to people south of the tree line by writing my nonfiction story about these amazing dogs.

When we visited Siu-Ling in Iqaluit, we took two of her puppies, Toko and Rohde, for a walk in the tundra. They looked like two

bouncy balls of fur darting here and there, curiously sniffing everything in their path. Toko and Rohde were incredibly cute, cuddly, and adorable, I could not help falling in love with these remarkable dogs and their captivating personalities.

I adopted Toko after he was retired from being a sled dog. When I took him for walks in Ottawa, people often stopped to ask me what kind of dog he was. I even had cars slow down and stop as the driver

Toko after his retirement.

rolled down his window to ask what kind of dog I had. One day, I met an elderly gentleman along the way who stopped to admire Toko and commented on what a magnificent dog he was. Toko was a former boss dog. He was indeed a magnificent example of a true Inuit Dog. His thick, mane-like fur and bearing gave him a regal appearance, and so, Toko became the inspiration for my book, later published as *The Canadian Inuit Dog: Icon of Canada's North*.

In my book, I wrote about the 2007 and 2008 Qimualaniq Quest in which Siu-Ling participated. She continued to live life to the fullest and enjoy her time in the serene Arctic with her beloved sled dogs and the many friends she'd made since moving there. They were part of what made her life worth living.

Siu-Ling and her dog team. (Photo credit: Ed Maruyama)

After completing my final writing assignment about the Inuit Dog in 2009, my personal ICL instructor, Jessica Lee Anderson, wrote: "I have to say that this was the most organized and polished nonfiction book assignment I've received to date! I hope you feel quite proud of yourself for the blood, sweat, and tears you've poured into this project. This book WILL find a home. It may take some patience, but it is deserving of publication."

However, I did not do anything with my manuscript until much later. It was summer, and the outdoors beckoned. I loved working in my garden and going hiking and biking. Those activities kept me going as I struggled with worry about my daughter's health and tried to keep a positive attitude. There were weddings and birthdays to attend and travel plans to make. I was too busy to work on my manuscript and stashed it in the back of my drawer for *later*. Besides, I needed a break from spending too much time in front of my computer.

After discussing dream trips with Debbie, Siu-Ling decided to go on a dogsledding journey along the east coast of Baffin Island to celebrate five cancer-free years. With help from a friend, Inuk hunter Ilkoo Angutikjuaq (*Inuk* is singular for a person of Inuit descent), Siu-Ling reviewed maps and Inuit hunting routes. Together with Matty McNair, they planned and executed the logistics needed to safely navigate challenging Arctic terrain and figured out where to place the food caches they would need along the 628-mile (1,010-kilometer) route.

Connie Maley, another friend from Calgary, joined Siu-Ling, Matty, and Debbie on this once-in-a-lifetime trip with 24 dogs. They started their journey from Qikiqtarjuaq on March 31, 2009.

Matty's team consisted of 14 dogs, while Siu-Ling had ten. Equipped with tents, supplies, and all necessities for such an impressive endeavor— including shotguns in case they came across polar bears — the teams skied their way between hummocks,

Siu-Ling on her 1000+ kilometer journey along the east coast of Baffin Island. Day 18 - April 19, 2009. (Photo credit: Debbie McCallister)

*Siu-Ling leading the team on her skis. Day 25 – April 26, 2009.
(Photo credit: Debbie McCallister)*

pressure ridges and leads on the sea ice and over bumpy, snow-covered terrain on the island. They trekked through all kinds of wind and weather for thirty days. It was a testament to Siu-Ling's strength, resilience, endurance,

Siu-Ling giving a pep talk to her team. Day 28 – April 29, 2009. (Photo credit: Debbie McCallister)

and the close bond she had with her dogs and her friends. After Siu-Ling managed to complete that 1000+ km dog sledding journey, six years after her cancer diagnosis, I tried not to worry about her health and pushed cancer out of my mind. She had surpassed the five-year mark as an ovarian cancer survivor and continued to live life to the fullest, making the most of every single day by always being thoughtful, kind, and considerate. She looked healthy and well, and that was what was most important to me.

Off to See the World

In 2011, Siu-Ling accompanied her dad and me on a trip to China, where we visited various UNESCO World Heritage sites, far from the standard tourist traps. We had never been to China before. This trip was a family adventure and an experience that introduced Siu-Ling to our Asian culture and heritage. One of the places we visited was Mount Emei, one of Buddhism's holiest sites dating back more than 1500 years. Rising more than 3000 meters above sea level, Mount Emei is the highest of four Buddhist mountains in China. Many of the temples on this mountain are dedicated to the Bodhisattva of Universal Benevolence, Puxian, who is said to have ascended to the top of the mountain on a six-tusked elephant during the 6th century. Being on this trip was a learning and enriching experience for all of us, and especially for Siu-Ling, as she learned about the home of her ancestors.

We took a cable car to the top of Mount Emei and, together, the three of us walked the rest of the way to the Golden Summit; it was shrouded in a heavy cloak of fog, creating a surreal atmosphere. Now and then, the sun attempted to penetrate the thick cloud ceiling, sending feeble gleams of light through the dense fog that surrounded this sacred mountain. Although it was a steep climb up slippery stone steps, the path was well-maintained. Siu-Ling always walked behind me to make sure I was alright. She commented on the Buddhist monks who were walking this pilgrim's trail with us. They wore American-brand running shoes instead of the traditional sandals under their flowing saffron robes. One stopped to chatter and text on his mobile phone. We chuckled when we saw how modern technology had even penetrated the inner sanctuary of this ancient order.

Upon reaching the Golden Summit, the statue of Puxian—at 48 meters (157.5 feet) tall, the tallest golden Buddha in the world—emerged through the dense fog like a ghostly apparition that took our breaths away. I noticed Siu-Ling standing in awe as she looked up at the giant Buddha. It made me wonder what she was thinking.

We also visited Zhangjiajie, one of China's most beautiful ancient mountain ranges, with its majestic quartz sandstone pillars, which are often depicted in mysterious-looking Chinese brush paintings. Zhangjiajie is a vast nature reserve that UNESCO designated as a World Heritage site in 1992. Siu-Ling, who had been reading about Zhangjiajie on her Blackberry, mentioned that this was the site James Cameron selected to film his epic movie *Avatar* (which means floating mountains).

One of the highlights of Zhangjiajie is Tianmen Shan, or Tianmen Mountain, the highest peak in Zhangjiajie known for its Heaven's Gate, an opening in the mountain large enough for planes to fly through. To get there, we took what is considered the longest and fastest cable car in the world, covering a distance of 7.5 km (4.66 miles) and rising to the height of 1279 m (4196 feet)! Zipping up the mountain in a glass-enclosed cabin, high above the ground, through the dense fog, between natural stone pillars crowned with bonsai trees

Siu-Ling with her dad and me in China in 2011.

took our breaths away! All Siu-Ling said was, "Wow!" as she took in the awe-inspiring vista around us.

After reaching the end station, the three of us took a special bus up Tiongtian Avenue. This avenue has 99 dizzying, death-defying hairpin turns, symbolizing the nine palaces of Heaven. To the Chinese, it is the "Earth Landmark to God."

Siu-Ling wanted to know the significance of the number nine. Why 99 and 999? In Chinese culture, the number 9 stands for completeness and eternity. It symbolizes the supreme sovereignty of the emperor. To reach Heaven's Gate, we had to climb the Tianan Stairs, a set of stairs with 999 steps and no landings where we could stop and rest. Together, Siu-Ling and I challenged ourselves to climb the "Stairway to Heaven," while her dad stayed below to chat with friends who were on the same trip. I could hear my heart pumping in my ears as I struggled up the steep climb and tried to catch my breath. When we finally reached Heaven's Gate, we were rewarded with a spectacular view of the surrounding countryside. Siu-Ling and I imagined we were looking down from Heaven as we stood side by side to see the earth below. We were happy we had each other and pleased that we could tackle the 999 steep steps on the Stairway to Heaven as a team. It was the closest to Heaven we both had ever been.

In May 2013, my husband and I flew to Perth, Australia, for my nephew's wedding. I was so happy that Siu-Ling was able to come with us. She took care of our travel arrangements and made plans to explore Australia's west coast after the wedding. It was a comfort to have our daughter with us, as my husband and I were both in our seventies. Siu-Ling made sure her dad and I were well taken care of. We rented a car and, with Siu-Ling at the wheel, went on an unforgettable road trip. We visited the Pinnacles, with its unique natural limestone formations and drove past deserts along Western Australia's coast where we saw kangaroos hopping along the highway at dusk. We continued to Shark Bay Marine Park, a

The three of us in Australia in 2013.

world heritage area, and stayed in Monkey Mia, which is known for its dolphin-feeding station where visitors can interact with dolphins in their natural habitat. Monkey Mia is one of the largest non-invasive dolphin research sites in the world. As a biologist, Siu-Ling was interested in the Monkey Mia Dolphin Research Project, started in 1982. I often saw her talking to park rangers to find out more about the dolphins. Having Siu-Ling along made that trip extra special. It made us appreciate our loving, considerate, and kind daughter even more. Siu-Ling continued to warm our hearts and fill us with much love and gratitude.

An Unexpected Blow

Three months later, in August 2013, Siu-Ling had her ten-year check-up and was considered "cancer-free," as her CA-125, a tumor marker used in the diagnosis of ovarian cancer, was below the reference range of 35. She continued her work in the North, went on field trips to do research, spent time with her many friends, and cared for her beloved team of dogs.

One day she went to her doctor in Iqaluit for a knee injury and casually mentioned that she had this strange feeling in her stomach. She said it felt as if she had pulled a muscle but added that she was okay. The doctor, who was aware of her medical history, examined her and decided to order some tests. When her CA-125 test came back, it was alarmingly high. The doctor immediately arranged for Siu-Ling to see a gynecologist in Ottawa for a biopsy. Siu-Ling must have sensed that the cancer was back, even though she carried on as usual and did not make her suspicions known. I remember her saying there was no point in worrying about something which might be nothing.

Just before Christmas, we accompanied Siu-Ling to Ottawa General Hospital for the result of her biopsy. Siu-Ling, brother Jeff, her dad, and I were waiting in a private, dimly lit windowless waiting room in the doctor's office at the hospital. Somehow, being in that gloomy room with its oversized leather chairs and tissue box on the coffee table made us feel uncomfortable. None of us said much until one of us mumbled a mindless comment about the atmosphere in the room and the Kleenex box on the table. When the door opened, the ghost-like figure of the doctor in her white coat appeared like a bearer of gloom and doom. I held my breath and felt my heart sink into my stomach. I knew before she even spoke that cancer had reared its ugly head once again.

Calm and collected as always, Siu-Ling resolutely rose from her seat when the doctor entered and, before the doctor could say anything, she told her that, whatever the result of the biopsy, she did not want to know her prognosis. Like in 2003, when the surgeon told her she had cancer, she told this doctor that she wanted her to explain how to tackle whatever was in store. The doctor was temporarily taken aback, then visibly loosened up when she realized that she did not have to reveal the bad news.

Siu-Ling started chemotherapy a couple of weeks later, in January 2014. She came to Ottawa to stay with us for her treatment at Ottawa General Hospital. Before her second chemo session in February, she traveled to Alberta to go skiing with friends in the Rocky Mountains like she had done before. When she was feeling better between chemo treatments, she and I continued taking our dogs for walks, every single day. We went cross-country skiing on nearby nature trails as long as snow conditions allowed. Those mother and daughter times in nature were moments that filled my heart with love and gratitude. Just being with my daughter and making the most of our time together were precious to me. We walked and talked about all kinds of things and, again, Siu-Ling mothered her mother, leading the way on the ski trail and telling me to be careful when going down the next hill. To be with Siu-Ling made me feel safe and protected. I did not have to worry about getting lost, because she somehow always knew the way.

A Precious Gift

Siu-Ling always found joy in nature and our dogs' unbridled happiness whenever we let them run freely. Going for a walk in the forest with my daughter was fun. It also often became a learning experience when my daughter, the biologist, pointed things out to me that I would not have noticed or simply took for granted. "Look up!" she'd say, pointing to a bird circling in the sky. "That's a falcon."

"A falcon? How can you tell it's a falcon?"

"Falcons have long, slender wings that are pointed at the end," she explained, "whereas a hawk's wings are wider in relation to its body and usually have rounded ends."

She also used to point out the difference between pine, spruce, and fir, all of which belong to the genus *Pinaceae*, the pine family of conifers. To me, they all look the same, but upon closer examination of their needles, there is, indeed, a difference. I just have to remember which is which. There are more than 100 different species of pine trees. The ones we are most familiar with in Canada are in the white pine group. They have long, slender needles in groups of five. Needles that come in groups of two, three, or five belong to different kinds of pine trees. Needles that come off singly belong to either fir or spruce, but … how do you tell the difference between fir and spruce?

"If you pull off a needle that easily rolls between your fingers, it is spruce. If it is flat and does not roll easily, it's fir." Hmm, I must remember the F in Flat and Fir.

Winter made way for Spring and, at the end of her treatment, unlike the first time, chemotherapy did not have the hoped-for outcome. Despite our disappointment, I still had hope that my daughter would overcome this setback as she did before and that she would be alright. However, Siu-Ling was more realistic. She must have known things did not look good. To spare us the anxiety and heartache of a depressing prognosis, she did not share her concerns with us. Rather than brooding over it, Siu-Ling decided to make the most of the upcoming summer —while she still could. She was alive, and life was a precious gift that she wanted to enjoy.

CHAPTER 6

Living in the Moment

If you are depressed, you are living in the past.
If you are anxious, you are living in the future.
If you are at peace, you are living in the present.
~Lao Tzu

Siu-Ling bought her dream car, a Mercedes SUV, and planned to go on a road trip across Canada and south to Northern California to see the Redwood Forest. She discussed it with another close friend, Natalia, who was off work after she sustained a brain injury due to a collision on a ski hill. The two friends decided they should put their health challenges aside and find solace in nature by going camping in national parks in Canada and the United States.

Siu-Ling wanted to take her furry friend, Parker, along. Having him along would help them to pace themselves and remember to take it easy on their long car rides. It would make them stop at regular intervals to stretch their legs, rest, and go for a little walk before resuming their journey and finding a campsite before dark. Siu-Ling and Natalia, in spite of the challenges both were facing, chose to consciously deal with what was in the moment and focus on enjoying the good things in life.

Going on multiple-hour hikes to explore the natural wonders of Saskatchewan's Grassland National Park on their way out west was not an option for them. But I am sure they enjoyed its perfect environment for quiet contemplation in the park's well-known Dark Sky Preserve. The stars shine brightly there, where there is no light pollution, offering a magnificent display of a sparkling night sky that has been described as *celestial eye candy.*

Siu-Ling and Natalia also visited Oregon's Badlands Wilderness, with its breathtaking landforms and geologic features. They saw the Painted Hills, one of Oregon's Seven Wonders, with its millions of years of history visible in the layers of vibrant yellows, gold, blacks, and reds of the earth. Natalia said that *it was part of their reality* that they were not able to go on extensive hikes to explore the area. That did not mean they could not enjoy the solitude, view, and ecology of the Badlands Wilderness and marvel at the wonders of nature. The variety of wildlife species that inhabit the area and the fascinating fossils going back to the dinosaur era were things that interested Siu-Ling, the biologist, and Natalia, the paleontologist. Together, these two friends shared their experiences of going through the challenges each faced and their commitment to making the most out of life.

Before getting to California to see the Redwood Forest, their primary destination, they stopped at Crater Lake National Park, with its diverse wilderness and breathtaking beauty. Crater Lake is the deepest and one of the most beautiful lakes in the United States because of its intense blue color. It was formed 7,700 years ago, after the fierce eruption of Mount Mazuma triggered the mountain's collapse — another wonder of nature they just had to see.

It was Siu-Ling's dream to experience the magic of Northern

Siu-Ling and Natalia on their 1000+ mile trip to the Redwood Forest.

California's stunning Redwood National Park and see some of the tallest trees in the world while she still could — and she did. Unfortunately, Siu-Ling and I somehow did not talk much about the details of that trip, except that standing in front of one of those giant trees, some of which are more than 1,000 years old, was humbling and, as she said, enough to make her feel small and insignificant.

When I later asked Natalia about that trip, she told me what *an awesome trip* it was. They laughed a lot and found joy in shared experiences and their friendship. She said their road trip was a *joyful trip*. To be able to find joy in the face of their challenges is awe-inspiring. Isn't that what being alive is all about?

In spite of life's up and downs, they were able to recognize and find joy and gratitude. Joy for being able to make this amazing, once-in-a-lifetime trip and experience the wonders of nature, and gratitude for a friendship based on mutual understanding, shared interests, and a belief in always seeing their glasses as half full. Life is a precious gift that should be cherished in spite of its challenges. In the back of my mind, I somehow worried and wondered at the time if this trip might have also been a final goodbye to the friends she visited along the way.

Another Challenge

In the meantime, her team of oncologists in Ottawa arranged for her to enter a clinical trial at Princess Margaret Hospital in Toronto, one of the top five cancer research centers in the world. I accompanied Siu-Ling to Toronto on her first visit to the hospital for tests, to meet the oncologist, and schedule upcoming treatments. Siu-Ling loved driving, and we drove to Toronto in her new car, enjoying the autumn scenery along the highway and the cooler temperatures of an October day, as autumn had done her magic and transformed nature into a blazing kaleidoscope of color. Dear friends of Siu-Ling's, Amy and Marcus, generously offered their apartment in Toronto for us to stay in while they were away. After an overnight stay and Siu-Ling's appointments at the hospital, we drove back to Ottawa full of renewed hope for a recovery.

When Siu-Ling started treatment in Toronto, she took the train from Ottawa every three weeks. I offered to accompany her, but she preferred to go alone, both to assert her independence and because she did not want to be a burden. Being on her own also allowed her to spend time with friends in Toronto and go out for dinner before going to the hospital for chemo the next morning. After treatment, she would go straight to the station and take the train for an almost five-hour trip back home to us. Traveling back and forth between Ottawa and Toronto for treatment every three weeks was a challenge, but she did it. In spite of our heavy hearts, we all admired her for her resilience and the strength of her character. Our Siu-Ling was such a trooper.

The first couple of treatments gave us renewed hope, but the results from the remaining treatments in early 2015 dashed our hope for her recovery. It was heartbreaking. Little did I know her cancer had spread. Siu-Ling quietly kept it to herself. After completion of the clinical trial, her oncologists prescribed radiation, another assault on her body. By that time, my mind had grown numb. I drove her to the hospital for radiation treatments and appointments, but I was not aware of the severity of the illness that was quietly ravaging her body. After she finished radiation treatments, Siu-Ling still got up to walk the dogs every single day. She went to the gym with Natalia, met friends for lunch or coffee, went cross-country skiing with me, and traveled back and forth between Ottawa and her home in Iqaluit to visit with friends, check on her beloved dogs, and go dog sledding.

Creating a Legacy

During this time, Siu-Ling urged me to polish up my manuscript about the Inuit Dog and find a publisher. She offered to review what I had written and invited me to visit her in Iqaluit to meet her dogs and her dog-teaming friends. I met her old friend, Matty McNair, who led the first women-only expedition to the North Pole in 1998 and had been on the East-Baffin journey with Siu-Ling, Debbie, and Connie in 2009.

Siu-Ling arranged for me and her dad to fly to Kimmirut, a traditional Inuit hamlet on the southernmost peninsula of Baffin Island, just across the Hudson Strait, to interview Elijah Padluq, a well-known Inuk elder who used to travel with his team of dogs to go hunting. Siu-Ling also arranged for her Inuk friend, Kathy Martha Padluq,

Elijah's daughter, to accompany us so she could introduce us to her parents and do the translations, because Elijah only spoke Inuktitut.

I learned a lot from Elijah and Siu-Ling's dog-teaming friends, many of whom have lived and run dogs in Iqaluit for decades. Siu-Ling had also arranged for me to meet with Ken MacRury, who lived and worked in Iqaluit, where he'd owned a team of Inuit Dogs for decades. Ken is an authority on Inuit Dogs. He had written his Master's thesis on this amazing aboriginal landrace and was a great help to me. He reviewed my manuscript multiple times and made many valuable suggestions and corrections based on his extensive knowledge and experience with the awe-inspiring Canadian Inuit Dogs. I also have Siu-Ling to thank for introducing me to Sue Hamilton, owner, publisher, and editor of The Fan Hitch website. Sue also published a print edition of the Inuit Sled Dogs International (ISDI) journal and shared all kinds of information and scholarly articles that she'd published on her website with me. She also reviewed my manuscript time after time. My book would not have been what it is without help from Siu-Ling, Ken MacRury, and Sue Hamilton. I also received invaluable help from Siu-Ling's kind and experienced dog-teaming friends, as well as her friend Bill Carpenter, who is known for saving the Inuit Dog from extinction

I was lucky when I found Revodana Publishing, a niche publisher of books about ancient dogs. I contacted Revodana and spoke with Denise Flaim, Revodana's publisher and editor, after which she offered me a contract. I was so happy that Siu-Ling was still able to see my contract and hold it in her hands. After she read it, she put her arms around me and told me how happy and proud she was of me.

CHAPTER 7

One Last Time

I wonder what it feels like to do something
and know it's for the last time?
~Kim Han

After I submitted my manuscript to Revodana Publishing, we went through the editing process. In the meantime, Siu-Ling's condition had deteriorated. However, she continued to live life to the fullest and help me with my book. She even traveled to Alberta and British Columbia to visit friends and ski in the Canadian Rockies, like she had done almost every year since she moved to Iqaluit in 1998. It was as if she had to do it just *one last time*.

In February 2016, Siu-Ling visited two of her closest friends, Susan Simm and Dan McAllister. They own a condo in Sun Peaks Ski Resort, the second largest ski area in Canada's Rocky Mountains. When they picked Siu-Ling up from the airport in Kamloops, a city in British Columbia, Dan and Susan saw, with a sinking heart, that

Siu-Ling was not well. Upon arrival at their condo, Siu-Ling went to bed but insisted that she was going to go skiing after. It was late afternoon when Dan took her out for a short cross-country ski outing. They did not go far. Susan estimated 200 meters (656 feet), but it was something Siu-Ling had to do. Dan and Susan were *extremely worried* about Siu-Ling and tried to convince her to go to the Medical Centre, but Siu-Ling refused. She said she would ask her friend, Vamini Selvanandan, a family physician and friend in Banff, to check her when she arrived there. Banff is a municipality in Banff National Park in Alberta, almost 500 km (≈310 miles) from Kamloops.

After a day or two, when Siu-Ling felt a little better, she told Susan she felt like skiing a downhill run. She looked a bit better but was still moving very slowly. Susan and Dan let her take her time getting ready. In the meantime, they went skiing, agreeing that Siu-Ling would join them when she finished her preparations. Again, this was something Siu-Ling had to do … one last time.

Susan told me that ski run took a long, long time. Siu-Ling managed to ski three loops, then collapsed and had to lie down in the snow, feeling utterly drained and sick with exhaustion. Susan accompanied her on that run and stood behind her at all times to protect her from oncoming skiers. She said it was *brutal* and *very upsetting*. I am so sorry Susan had to experience that part of Siu-Ling's life. I did not realize how bad it was. It broke my heart to learn how hard Siu-Ling tried to keep up with life in the shadow of death. She longed to do the things she used to do, the things she loved, just one more time, despite her delicate condition. It is a testament to the strength of her spirit, her resolve, courage, and the kind of person she was. As one of her doctors said, it was *humbling*.

After that last run, Susan said they both went back to the condo for Siu-Ling to rest. Again, Susan tried to persuade Siu-Ling to see a doctor, but Siu-Ling said she would wait until she saw Vamini.

When it was time for Siu-Ling to fly to Banff, Susan had a hard time hiding her concern about her friend's well-being. When she and Dan put Siu-Ling on the plane, they saw that she could barely lift her luggage. Siu-Ling, who was so strong and could easily carry a canoe all by herself, no longer had the strength to pick up her suitcase. When they said goodbye, Susan told Siu-Ling to text her as soon as she arrived in Banff. It was Vamini who took Siu-Ling to the hospital in Banff for a blood transfusion after she examined her and did a couple of tests.

As Tim later said in his eulogy, during one of Siu-Ling's last meetings with the oncologist at the hospital in Ottawa, the doctor remarked how shocked she was that Siu-Ling had the strength to even make it to the hospital. She said patients with Siu-Ling's hemoglobin count normally couldn't even sit up in bed. When the doctor asked Siu-Ling to describe her days, the first thing Siu-Ling said was, "Well, I get up and take the dogs for a walk …" The doctor apparently was so stunned she almost fell off her chair. Siu-Ling's ability to soldier on was truly remarkable. She defied all expectations. In a disease that takes many women in weeks, months, or a limited number of years, Siu-Ling lasted more than 13 years! When she should have been in bed, she was out skiing with me, hiking in the nearby forest, or walking the dogs.

Being outdoors was restorative to Siu-Ling and, as an outdoor person, nature soothed her soul. In one of her journals, I found the following quote which she wrote in March 1993, long before cancer was on anyone's mind: *Days of being outside under beautiful conditions really make me relish life and how good things are.*

Life in the Arctic had a profound impact on Siu-Ling that made her feel humble. She often expressed her observations and feelings about people, nature, and life in sketches, poems, and songs. Here is one such poem:

This is a very powerful land.
There is strength in its silence.
The animals possess it still, being not interlopers,
Being yet a part of it.
I revel in what it gives, and in what it takes.
It lies heavy upon me, me so small.
But it is only here that I can fly,
Torn from my chest
Like a geyser, only cold and cutting sprays,
Not warm steam and hot.

I lie back, overwhelmed by the land
As it rolls over me, onto me, into me.
Mountains and light
Ice and fog
Tundra and stone.
Ocean, wind, roaring.
I almost die.
Choking on my tears, choking on my heart.
It captures me, tears me in half.
But I am never scattered, though I spiral and explode.

When Jeff shared that poem with Shannon Hessian, one of Siu-Ling's closest friends, she wrote: "How she amazes me; how I wish I could talk to her. I truly think she is an ancient soul brought here to earth to share wisdom during her time with us and beyond … I am grateful."

CHAPTER 8

Time to Say Goodbye

Don't cry because it's over. Smile because it happened.
~Dr. Seuss

One of the songs on the album Siu-Ling recorded as part of her legacy is called "Home." She wrote it for her good friend, Pierre, one of the musicians who accompanied her on her album. Pierre used to live in Iqaluit before he moved to Ottawa. Siu-Ling knew how much Pierre loved and missed the Arctic, just like she did. She wrote the following song that describes the Arctic, as seen through her eyes:

Where I am, the sun just keeps going 'round
At night it may dim, but it don't quite go down
And until the world tilts, we roll into the darkness
So we'll sleep till the sun comes back and travel closer to home.

Where I am, we all can walk on the ocean
And everyone can see where the sky meets the land
And life up here is an act of devotion
It lets you fly or lets you down
But it don't hold your hand

Where I am, the ground gives back your walking
The silence it roars and the distance can lie
Where I am, the wind can steal all your talking
But still when we walk away, we just don't say goodbye.

In the Spring of 2016, Siu-Ling paid one last trip to her home in Iqaluit. She'd lived there for eighteen years and traveled all over the island with her team of dogs. Jeff came with her, and together they visited the dogs and went dogsledding as often as they could. After their last outing, as they were getting ready to leave, one of the dogs suddenly let out a mournful howl. A chorus of his teammates soon joined him. They howled with an eeriness that echoed across the frozen tundra. Jeff said it sent chills up his spine.

Her friend Dan from Calgary visited Siu-Ling in Iqaluit shortly after Jeff left. Together, Siu-Ling and Dan went dogsledding, a pastime she was passionate about. After their last outing, Siu-Ling's dogs started howling again as Siu-Ling and Dan were getting ready to leave. Inuit Dogs are known to have a sixth sense, and the dogs knew they would never see Siu-Ling again.

A couple of weeks later, Siu-Ling flew to the United Kingdom to visit brother Tim and his family in London one last time. From London, she flew to the Netherlands, where our family was having a small reunion. We all stayed at my sister's house just outside Groningen. My brother and his wife came from Jakarta, Indonesia; their daughter and her family flew in from Perth, Australia, and my husband and I from Canada. It was a joy to see family we had not seen in many years.

We did some sightseeing in the area and visited Giethoorn, a peaceful, picturesque village known as "Dutch Venice," because instead of streets, there are canals and waterways. We went on a canal cruise, gently gliding along small canals past old but pretty thatched-roof farmhouses. It was during this trip that I noticed how much Siu-Ling had slowed down. While she normally would have been the leader of the pack, this time, I saw with trepidation how hard she tried to keep up with the rest of the family. During the next couple of days, I noticed how she spent more time in bed and did not eat much. I tried not to worry, but it was as if long, icy fingers were reaching out to take my daughter away from me, giving me chills and a nagging ache in my heart that made me feel sick to my stomach.

Siu-Ling was scheduled to fly back to Ottawa on July 3 to begin chemotherapy with a different kind of drug. My sweet niece Suzanna, a physician, had arranged for Siu-Ling's flight home to be upgraded to business class, so she would be comfortable and well-taken care of during the long flight. My husband flew back to Ottawa to be with her. I stayed behind because it was going to be my sister's 70th birthday on the weekend. Unfortunately, I was not meant to stay and celebrate that milestone with her. My husband called from Ottawa to say that Siu-Ling could not begin the chemotherapy on July 5, as scheduled, and that the doctors had decided to keep her in the hospital to conduct some tests. Alarm bells rang in my head and, instead of staying till the weekend for my sister's birthday, I decided to fly straight home to Ottawa.

Siu-Ling's Legacy

Upon arrival in Ottawa, my husband Bing, Jeff, and his family were waiting for me. We drove straight to the hospital to see Siu-Ling. When we arrived at the hospital, we went up to her room. We peeked in and saw her sitting by the window, dressed in a hospital gown. She was hooked up to an intravenous device and somehow looked so small and fragile. Dusk had fallen. The only light in the room came from the street and parking lot lights below her window. City lights flickered in the distance, indicating there was life outside that dim and dreary hospital room. When we entered the room, she looked up and smiled that lovely smile of hers that brightened up her face. We hugged her carefully, to avoid disturbing the drip line attached to the Peripherally Inserted Central Catheter (PICC) line on her arm.

"You came back!" she said, happily. "I thought you were going to stay for auntie's birthday."

"No, I wanted to be with you," I said as I stroked her arm.

As always, she was the first to ask how I was and if I had a good flight. After that, she came right to the point and told us matter-of-factly that the doctors had told her there was nothing more they could do and that she only had a few weeks to live. She was calm and composed. I could not believe what I heard. The shock of this unbelievable news numbed me, making me unable to react, while my husband, her stoic dad, broke down as he put his arms around her and cried, "I am going to miss you!"

Siu-Ling patted her dad to comfort him and said, "I know. It is okay, Dad. Don't cry." Leaning back in her chair, she then said, "Don't be sad ... There is something I am leaving you." I stared at her, having no idea what she was talking about.

"What do you mean?" I stammered mindlessly.

"My music," she said calmly. "My friends produced a CD of my music."

"What music?" That's when she told us that she had written a whole repertoire of songs. We knew she loved music, because we often heard her quietly playing the guitar. We had no idea she had been writing music, because she had been keeping it to herself, but, as it turned out, music was what made Siu-Ling tick.

She had continued taking recorder lessons for several years after we moved to Ottawa and participated in music festivals there, where she always won prizes. When she started grade 7, she took up the flute, which she played in the school band throughout middle and high school. When she was 11, she also took two semesters of formal piano lessons but was mostly self-taught. I was amazed to hear her play Beethoven's *Piano Sonata, Pathétique*, and other classical pieces by heart as if she had been playing the piano for years.

Little did we know that Siu-Ling had been, as she later said, "privately incubating *stuff*." When Robert Aubé, a close friend and professional musician living in Iqaluit, first discovered Siu-Ling's music, he said, "When I heard her first song, I was blown away!" He insisted that it was okay to call her *stuff* songs, real songs, and that her music should be shared. Rob, who plays the upright bass, became the driving force and, as Siu-Ling said, the "project manager extraordinaire" in the production of her music, with help from other professional musicians: Jeff Maurice (rhythm guitar), Pierre Lecomte (multi-instrumentalist), Jamal Shirley (lead guitar), Emily Woods (back-up vocals), Steve Rigby (drums), Gina Burgess (violin), and Inuk throat singer, Nancy Mike. Were it not for Rob's sense of urgency to move this project forward, it would not have come together as quickly as it had, if at all. Little did anybody know how justified his sense of urgency was, for nobody knew that Siu-Ling's life on earth was ebbing away. As Siu-Ling later said about the CD, "I love that this project has grown from our friendship." Rob worked day and night to put it all together. The CD was professionally recorded and mixed at Siku Music Studio in Iqaluit by Jeff Maurice and at Royal Mountain Studios in Toronto by Nyles Misczyk. It was mastered by Chris Coleman at Nuvu Studio, Iqaluit. We owe Rob and all the musicians our deepest gratitude for capturing and preserving Siu-Ling's voice and beautiful music. When the CD was launched, August 20, 2016, Siu-Ling was interviewed by CBC's Sima Sahar Zerehi, who told the story of how Siu-Ling's album *To Those That Would Show Kindness* came into being.

CHAPTER 9

So Much Love

What we once deeply loved, we can never lose.
For all that we love deeply becomes a part of us.
~Helen Keller

That July evening when Siu-Ling was in the hospital, she called her friend Susan who owns the condo at Sun Peaks to tell her about her prognosis. Susan immediately said she could be in Ottawa in a few days if that was what Siu-Ling wanted. "Yes, please, come," Siu-Ling pleaded. Susan told me that, during that visit in Ottawa, Siu-Ling asked a mutual friend, Paul Crowley, a dear friend of Siu-Ling's, if he would ask Susan if she would be willing and able to stay *as long as possible* to help manage things, as she must have known that our lives had been turned upside down. Siu-Ling asked Paul to ask Susan because she knew Susan would not have been able to say *no* if she had asked her herself. Having Paul ask Susan gave Susan a way to decline if she couldn't stay. Siu-Ling knew it was asking a lot of a friend who lived thousands of miles away, where she had a husband

and a job managing his business. But she also knew that Susan was the person she trusted and could depend on to support the family and manage the difficult situation on this journey that was nearing its end. She was not worried about herself, but it was us she was concerned about. Even though she was dying, she wanted to ensure that we, her family, had the loving support of her many friends who graciously embraced us in their loving care. Siu-Ling once told us that when she was gone, our family would not diminish; instead, it would grow, because her closest friends would be there for us and become part of our family, and so it is.

As news of Siu-Ling's imminent demise spread like wildfire after she came home from the hospital on July 8, we were inundated with hundreds of visits from family, friends, and colleagues who came from all over Canada, the U.S., and Europe to visit her. Siu-Ling was excited and happy to see each and every one of them. "This is so exciting!" she exclaimed joyfully. "It's fun to see friends I haven't seen in a long time. It's almost like getting ready for a wedding, except, uh, heh heh, … this is not a wedding," she said with a chuckle.

Debbie, Siu-Ling's physician friend who went on the 1000+ km dogsledding trip along the east coast of Baffin Island with Siu-Ling, had become very close to Siu-Ling. She started organizing Siu-Ling's care from her home in Calgary to ensure that she would be able to approach the end of her life with dignity and grace, surrounded by the love of family and friends. It was Siu-Ling's wish to spend her last couple of weeks at home with family instead of in a hospital or hospice. She wanted to be home with us and, as she said, *hear and smell the sounds and scents of home* and feel the love and comfort of being home, surrounded by the people she loved.

Debbie started organizing Siu-Ling's care by contacting colleagues in hospitals in Iqaluit, where Siu-Ling had resided for many years, and in Ottawa, where she wanted to be. She guided and instructed Susan, who also lives in Calgary, on what to do. It involved creating Reciprocity Agreements between provinces regarding Siu-Ling's care, as she was a resident of Nunavut, not Ontario. There were questions to ask of Siu-Ling's medical team regarding palliative care in Ottawa. Susan was to contact the on-call doctors, follow up on the results of her blood work, transfusions, and any care Siu-Ling would need. Susan knew Siu-Ling well and knew what Siu-Ling liked and disliked. During this time, Siu-Ling arranged for Susan to manage the day-to-day comings and goings of our topsy-turvy existence, in an effort to maintain some control of her life. Susan willingly agreed and told me she regarded it as a *job* that she took *very seriously,* to the point that she sometimes felt she was missing out on those final weeks with Siu-Ling because she had a lot on her plate, but, she said, she has memories from that time that allowed her to *let go of that.*

During their brief, one-on-one early morning talks, Siu-Ling told Susan, who stayed at our home to be close to Siu-Ling, that she wished she had not skimped on dipping lobster in lots of melted butter whenever we had a lobster dinner on our camping trips in Nova Scotia. Susan then told Siu-Ling that it was something she could remedy. It so happened Susan was planning to visit her family in Nova Scotia. She took that opportunity to bring back a dozen live lobsters so Siu-Ling would be able to enjoy an authentic Nova Scotia lobster dinner and dip her lobster in lots of melted butter. It warmed my heart to see how much Siu-Ling's friends loved her and would do anything to make her happy.

That evening, we all had a delicious lobster dinner with bowls of melted garlic butter, fresh corn on the cob, and homemade buns which Lynn Peplinski, another very close friend of Siu-Ling's, baked in our kitchen. Siu-Ling savored the delicious dinner as she reminisced about our memorable family camping trips in Nova Scotia every August. It was the last dinner she enjoyed.

Susan said *the most powerful memory* she had of Siu-Ling was when all of us were seated at the dinner table that night. Siu-Ling sat to Susan's left. When she dipped a chunk of lobster in a bowl of melted butter, she looked at Susan with affection, gratitude, and *that Siu-Ling smile,* and said, "Thank you, Susan." The look on Siu-Ling's face and those three little words touched her deeply.

Reminiscing about the current summer, Siu-Ling said, "It's a pretty amazing summer, traveling to the U.K. and Holland to be with family I have not seen in years, being home with *my love people,* the many visits from friends I have not seen in ages, the food, the snacks … It's so amazing," she chuckled, "aside from the fact that I am dying …."

In a note to Shannon Hessian, one of her closest friends, Siu-Ling wrote:

"It's actually been quite a fun several weeks with my nearest and dearest hanging about just getting to know one another (my brothers and parents and some of my closest friends are getting a lot of bonding time – there are lots of meals and excursions (other than having an entourage take me to a silly movie, I don't go on the excursions), a bit of music (the whole CD thing is such a shock to me, but it's a fun element), and me shuffling around the house like a queen (for the first time in my life not feeling the need to be independent) and just asking for things (every little whim being met,

at least I haven't asked for anyone to hand feed me peeled grapes yet). Not that there aren't tears (but most are being kept from dripping all over me), but it's quite an experience of being fully in the moment and enjoying the love and support, and just plain goodness in everyone's heart. It is much helped by the fact that, despite the cold truth of my failing health, I am still totally lucid, and I am not in any pain."

During one long weekend in August, Robert, Pierre, and a couple of other friends involved with Siu-Ling's musical CD, brought their musical instruments to our house when they came to see Siu-Ling. Despite our heavy hearts, music, song, and laughter filled the air and streamed out our open windows, mingling with the sweet scents of a sunny summer day. That's when Siu-Ling said: "I know I'm dying, but I am having such a great summer." When Errol, another musician friend, and Emily who sang the back-up vocals on the CD, started singing Leonard Cohen's *Hallelujah* accompanied by Rob and Pierre on their guitars, Errol tapped the beat to this melancholy melody on a small drum, while Emily shook the maracas. If sadness can be beautiful, this was such a moment. It tore at my heart strings, but when Siu-Ling picked up her guitar and started singing one of her compositions, *I Am With You Everywhere,* accompanied by Rob and Pierre, there wasn't a dry eye in the room.

I Am With You Everywhere

> *You always shine*
> *Like the diamonds in the snow*
> *You'll be the warmth*

In the sunrise casting gold
You are the brightness
That flames in autumn leaves
You are the freedom
Of a cool escarpment breeze

And you will glide beside me on the ridge
And surf the breaking waters 'neath the bridge
And though I seem to lose you in the hills,
It's at the lookout I can find you still

You whisper soft like the wind among the pines
I dream your smile, dream everything is fine
I hear you sing in the mountains high and free
I hear you laugh in the roaring of the sea

I see the sky that is mirrored in the lake
The mountain dawn that calls me to awake
The dancing fire 'round which we all draw near
The ones you love will always keep you here

Chorus:
Everywhere you are
Everywhere I am,
Everywhere we'll be
We'll always be together,
We'll always be together, yes, we will.

I believe this song was meant to comfort those of us who love and miss her. Siu-Ling always found comfort and joy in nature. And so, it is in nature where she wanted us to see her when she's gone. Everywhere we are, everywhere she is, *everywhere we'll be, we'll always be together, yes, we will.*

Throughout the next couple of weeks, our house was inundated with visits from friends who put their lives on hold and jumped on planes from across the world to visit Siu-Ling for a final farewell. It was heartwarming to see the number of friends who made an effort to travel to Ottawa from wherever they lived. Brother Tim, who flew in from London with our two grandchildren, became the social secretary, scheduling visits with the hundreds of friends, family members, and colleagues who came to see Siu-Ling. One friend flew in from Toronto one early afternoon and flew back the same evening after her visit. Friends and family catered to Siu-Ling and looked after her, surrounding her with so much love. Debbie came all the way from Calgary every other weekend to be with Siu-Ling, check on her, and make sure she was well taken care of. Debbie took turns with Susan, who also came every other week, so that one of them was always here.

Jeff and Tim administered Siu-Ling's meds with help from cousin Suzanna, a physician who came from Holland to be with Siu-Ling. Looking back, it warms my heart with love and gratitude to both Debbie and Susan, who took turns flying back and forth between their work in Calgary and their loving friendship for Siu-Ling in Ottawa. Somebody commented how expensive it must be for Siu-Ling's friends to travel back and forth to Ottawa every weekend, while others flew in from out of the country. Another chuckle from Siu-Ling as she tilted her head, put up one finger, and said with a mischievous glint in her eyes, "I have rich friends."

Debbie, an anesthesiologist, pain physician, and pediatric palliative care physician, was Siu-Ling's confidante with whom she discussed her medical needs. They discussed every potential clinical trial, all options for a cure, but in January 2016, when they knew that the cancer had spread, their conversations changed. As Siu-Ling's health took a turn for the worse, they discussed Siu-Ling's hopes and goals, something I was not aware of at the time. Debbie taught Siu-Ling the art of self-hypnosis for pain and nausea management. She said, "Siu was an absolute master at the technique and, right to her last day, was able to control the pain signals into her brain and largely block the pain through hypnosis techniques, thereby minimizing the amount of pain medication that she needed at the end of life AND maintaining her beautiful sharp functioning brain. On my part, this was a work of love for Siu – I was so proud of her mastery and ability to control her own physiology – conserving energy – controlling pain." In a telephone conversation I had with Debbie, she said, "The power of Siu-Ling's brain was humbling."

In the meantime, Susan did a great job managing and organizing Siu-Ling's care and our upside-down, topsy-turvy lives. Lynn stayed with us and helped take care of the family, as she tended to Siu-Ling and did whatever she could to help. Every person who came to visit or stay with us provided Siu-Ling with so much love and care.

When Kina, Jeff and Diane's daughter, was a little girl, she affectionately nicknamed her auntie Siu-Ling, *Er*, short for Erla. I don't know how she came up with that name, but we all had special pet names for each other. Kina dearly loved her Auntie Er and visited every day to be with Siu-Ling. She learned how to flush Siu-Ling's PICC line and bought her different essential oils with her own money to help relieve pain, nausea, and anxiety. Kina lovingly massaged Siu-Ling every day to help make her feel better. Before giving her a massage, Kina always asked which essential oil she would like. I was touched to learn how much my granddaughter loved her Auntie Er and how much they meant to each other.

Cousin Andy, who came from Holland, knew how much Siu-Ling loved getting massages. He arranged for Siu-Ling's massage therapist, Wendy Parker, to come to the house every couple of days to give Siu-Ling a massage. Siu-Ling loved Wendy's gentle, soothing massages, which helped her to relax and release the tension in her body.

I was touched to see how gently and lovingly her brothers, Jeff and Tim, treated their sister and spoke to her as they helped her get out of bed. Siu-Ling only had to say she felt like having gelato or one of her favorite childhood candies she had not had in a long time and right away, Diane, Jeff's wife, would make an effort, driving all over town, if necessary, to get it.

Siu-Ling said she felt like a queen. In the meantime, I continued to be in a daze and just went through the motions, day after day, detached from the happenings around me—a means of self-preservation before the inevitable would crush me and shatter my soul.

Siu-Ling thought of everything. She had made sure her effects were in order and said she was *ready* and looking forward to her next *adventure* to find out what was *on the other side*. She said she'd been to places many could only dream of, done things she always wanted to do, and created memories with friends and family that nobody could take away. She was calm and composed and said she had no regrets about the life she had lived. The only regret she had was when she told me, with tears in her eyes, that she would not be able to look after her dad and me in our old age and that she was not able to give us grandchildren. "I had such a wonderful childhood," she said. "I wish I could have had children for you to love the way you loved me." Those words touched me very deeply. The Bible says for everything, there's a season and a time for every matter under heaven. Was looking after my daughter, being there for her as she approached the end of her life, the reason why I came back from the brink of death when Siu-Ling was three years old?

Siu-Ling believed in a higher power that decides the course of our lifetime on earth. Some people live to be a hundred, others live only years, days, or merely minutes. In her song, *Jane Said*, she wrote:

Jane said something about leaving
How the hardest moments are just before you're gone
And I've learned a little about grieving
Just when you think it's over,
You find it's never really gone.

I knew you'd be leaving
I knew that you'd have to go someday
But I kept denying that you couldn't stay
And Bob said something 'bout no crying
But there's just no denying
Sometimes you've got to shed those tears
And I've learned a little about dying
There's just no way of knowing
If you've got minutes or got years

I knew you'd be leaving
You'd probably be the first to go
We turn to the sunlight
But life casts a long shadow

We had our much-loved Siu-Ling for fifty-three years, seven months and seven days. She filled our lives with love, joy, laughter, a quirky sense of humor, and wonderful words of wisdom. Siu-Ling was wise beyond her years, ever since she was a little girl. She was the person people turned to when they needed someone to talk to, a listening ear, and advice. She was a no-nonsense person who had an extraordinary way of creating deep and lasting friendships and bringing people together. As a wildlife biologist, Siu-Ling was instrumental in helping the Canadian Wildlife Service (CWS) sign an *Inuit Impact Benefit Agreement,* which was the first time such an agreement was signed between CWS and the Inuit of Nunavut. She also provided the primary push to have all Nunavut wildlife management authorities and communities gather around the same table from day one.

Her boss, Bruce MacDonald, wrote us a very touching letter, saying that Siu-Ling's "fingerprints and ideals are all over what CWS does in the North." He added that:

Siu-Ling never tired of her efforts to ensure that the North, including its people and its wildlife, were always well-represented at every opportunity. I don't need to tell you that your daughter was a very special person, you already know that. But I hope that you will take even a little comfort in knowing the lasting impact she left on wildlife management in Canada's North.

Siu-Ling cared deeply about people and, as one of her closest friends said, "Siu-Ling made time for people and didn't just flit in and out of people's lives. She touched a lot of people in significant ways" -- significant enough for her many friends and colleagues to travel hundreds and even thousands of miles to be at her side to say goodbye.

One of the recurring comments we heard from Siu-Ling's friends was how her gentle kindness and philosophical wisdom helped them see life from a different perspective, finding the positives in any situation. She helped people be less negative and taught them how to generate and nurture positive energy.

Jeff asked Siu-Ling why her friends were such great people. There was not a jerk among them. She just shrugged and told him to see the good in everyone. She proved that you'll get back whatever you put out into this world.

Siu-Ling always saw her glass as half full. Despite her serious illness, she said, *there are not enough words to thank everyone that has made my life so full, so joyful, so rich with laughter and adventure.*

I am trying very hard to follow in her footsteps, see my glass as half full and turn a blind eye to the emptiness she left behind. Yes, my glass is only half full, but even in my deepest sorrow, I am thankful for the joy, happy times, and memories we shared as a family, and for having had this precious person for a daughter—a daughter who was loving, thoughtful, considerate, kind, and caring. Not only was she our daughter, she also was my best friend, a guiding light who lit up our lives and those of many others. Siu-Ling was an inspiration and, as we discovered, a talented musician and lyricist. She left us a musical legacy, thanks to her many friends in Iqaluit and, especially, Rob Aubé and Pierre Lecomte, two friends who convinced her that the beautiful music and lyrics she created should be shared. Our family thanks Rob, Pierre, and Jeff Maurice for preserving Siu-Ling's voice and music, and for creating the album of Siu-Ling's songs, *To Those Who Would Show Kindness*.

It broke our hearts to let her go, but we have to be thankful that we had her in our lives. She accomplished more at her young age than many do even in a long life. She never said much about her work, for she knew how to separate work from her day-to-day life, but I know that as a wildlife biologist working in Canada's Arctic, she built bridges between Inuit and government bureaucracy.

Siu-Ling playing the guitar. (Photo credit: Pierre Lecomte)

Siu-Ling left us with the beautiful music and songs she wrote that will always be a comfort to those who love and admire her. We were deeply touched by her observations of life and people in the

Arctic, which she described in her songs, notes, and drawings. We are grateful to her many friends who supported Rob and Pierre in the creation of the album which is a legacy of her wisdom, insight, love, and kindness. In spite of her illness, Siu-Ling did not stop caring. It was her wish that all proceeds from her CD support youth mental health initiatives in Nunavut. I hope we'll be able to keep helping those young people who desperately need help.

Life's Lessons

In his eulogy, Jeff wrote that when Siu-Ling lived in downtown Ottawa, she used to walk past a panhandler on Elgin Street every day. She would slip him a couple of dollars and a kind word from time to time, but one day, she decided to take him for lunch. Siu-Ling found out who he was, where he had been, and what his story was. She saw the human being behind the glazed eyes and worn clothing. She saw *the goodness of this downtrodden person.*

When she was in high school, Siu-Ling was a member of the Outers' Club, a group of outdoor enthusiasts who focus on all kinds of outdoor activities throughout the year. On one of their school trips, Siu-Ling noticed one girl nobody ever spoke to. Although, as Siu-Ling put it, she was not the kind of kid she usually hung out with, she decided to approach that girl to get to know her. She was pretty surprised to discover how interesting that girl was. It was, as Jeff said, a lesson she tried to teach us, namely that *every person has a story and a cool side.*

Siu-Ling loved to write. She wrote about her observations and jotted down thoughts and ideas, sometimes accompanied by a quick sketch. As Jeff was writing his eulogy, he flipped through one of her journals and came across notes from one of her big Baffin Island dog sledding trips. On one page, she had notes and sketches about some of the wildlife she saw and pictures of different knots for setting up her tent. Jeff came across one page where she wrote how her toes had started to turn black from frostbite and how the nail on her third toe was about to come off. Siu-Ling never mentioned that part of the trip to any of us. The only thing she spoke of was the breathtaking beauty of the High Arctic and how lucky she was to be able to experience every moment of it. As Jeff said, *she only saw the good in everything*.

Jeff and Siu-Ling were best friends their entire lives. As children, they used to explore the area around the suburb we lived in just outside Ottawa on their bikes. One of the main roads in the area was a dusty dirt road going past farmlands. Like me, Jeff always felt safe when he was with Siu-Ling, because she always knew the way. She was the practical one, the planner. Jeff said he would have just taken a pack of Bazooka Joe gum as a snack when they were exploring the neighborhood, but Siu-Ling would bring sandwiches, juice in one of those old thermoses, and a treat. When she was ten, she taught her younger brother to take the time to sit in the shade at the end of some farmer's driveway and enjoy a snack instead of rushing past on their bikes. Jeff said it was a great life lesson, not just the snack part, but *taking the time to slow down end enjoy, really enjoy and cherish the moment*. An extra two minutes never hurt anyone.

Even though the pain of losing our Siu-Ling was immense and unbearable, we have to be thankful for the time we were blessed to have her as our daughter, sister, auntie, colleague, cousin, and friend. It broke our hearts to say goodbye to our beloved Siu-Ling when she left home to embark on her adventure into the Great Beyond.

In his eulogy, Tim wrote that Siu-Ling was a quiet force that knew no limits. She had so many facets of which she never spoke. To her brothers, Siu-Ling was always the wise one, the philosophical one. He was surprised to discover how many of her friends said the same. She was a guiding light, and many considered her a sage.

As the owner of a team of sled dogs for almost twenty years, Siu-Ling experienced the joy of having litters of newborn puppies and the sadness of losing beloved dogs over the years. She got to know her dogs well and once said that we should learn to live like a dog. She compared the loss of someone you love with a dog that lost its leg. "It will hurt at first, and it will never grow back but, eventually, the dog will learn to live without the leg he lost, and go out and have fun again, chasing balls and cuddling on the sofa with his owner. Every once in a while, he will remember that he only has three legs, but he will not let that limit or define his life."

Shannon who had flown in from Iqaluit to be with Siu-Ling in her last days wrote us following note that she read at Siu-Ling's celebration of life service. It was so beautiful I would like to share it with you:

"Siu-Ling gave us an incredible gift over the past couple of months. She allowed us to glimpse at a profoundly intimate phase of life's journey that we so rarely bring ourselves to consider, bringing us closer to her and to each other, and she did it with courage, grace, and incredible strength. Siu-Ling gave us song to ease us in our undeniable grief and it will lift us when we feel ourselves stumbling.

As Siu-Ling travels on and we say goodbye, may she not worry for us, as we will draw her energy from the rays in the sun, feel her in the cool rain, hear her voice in the wind that brushes our face, see her in the extraordinary of the rainbow, the northern lights and the mountains. We will welcome her when the moon is full, and we will see her slide down a beam and land in our dreams. But truly, friends, we all know that it is in the blizzards, the rough waters, and the storms of our lives that we will be wrapped in her embrace.

We will look for Siu-Ling soaring in the sky and in the gardens as her adventure continues. As we celebrate her life today, we know that she will meet us when we journey in another tomorrow beyond what we can see today."

CHAPTER 10

Our Broken Hearts Still Beat

The sorrow we feel when we lose a loved one is
the price we pay to have had them in our lives.
~Rob Liano

I can't believe she is gone! How can I go on living without her? She was a part of me. I carried her close to my heart, nurtured her, and breathed for her for nine months. Now there is a big hole in my heart, a cold emptiness that has drained my very soul. A parent is not supposed to outlive her child. They say that when your parents die, you lose your past. If your husband or wife dies, you lose your present but, when your child dies, you lose part of your future. It is against the nature of things, and yet it happens. I know I am not the only mother who has lost her child, but my grief is mine alone, and theirs is theirs alone. We all grieve the loss of our child in our own way, regardless of who we are, where we came from, what we believe in, and how we were brought up thinking about the subject of life and death. There are no words to describe the pain of losing a child, no matter how young or old she is. While I mourned the loss of my child, Jeff and Tim mourned the loss of their sister, and our three grandchildren mourned the loss of their much-loved auntie.

My husband, Siu-Ling's pragmatic dad, kept a stiff upper lip. He was the strong one. At least, he acted that way. He tried to comfort me by reminding me of a friend who was only 47 years old when she lost her battle with ovarian cancer after only three years. He said we should be grateful we had Siu-Ling for thirteen. However, there were moments when I saw how the loss of his first-born child suddenly hit him. The other day, he suddenly said, "Apple cheeks!" His voice was quivering, and he almost choked as tears welled up in his eyes.

"What about apple cheeks?" I asked. Trembling, he said, "Siu-Ling had apple cheeks when she was a little girl. I loved her rosy apple cheeks." It was time for me to be the strong one. There was no need for words. I just hugged him tightly and patted his back, trying to comfort him.

A couple of days after Siu-Ling passed away, I was rushed to the emergency room of the hospital with chest pain, shortness of breath, and dizziness. I was hyperventilating and confused. Medical staff did all kinds of tests but could not find anything wrong with my heart. My physical symptoms were later attributed to my broken heart. It is known as *Takotsubo cardiomyopathy* or broken heart syndrome. It is described as a weakening of the left heart ventricle, the heart's main pumping chamber. This symptom is usually attributed to severe emotional or physical stress, such as grief over losing a loved one. I felt like my heart had been clawed out of my chest and shredded into a thousand pieces.

Although I was not aware of it at the time, my body was telling me something was wrong. I longed for Siu-Ling with all my heart, talked to her in my mind, and tried to find a connection with her even though she was gone. I buried my nose in her clothes and breathed in whatever was left of her scent. I wore her clothes to feel her embrace and sprayed her perfume behind my ears and around me to make me feel she was near. She used to write long, chatty letters with a fountain pen rather than a ballpoint pen, telling me stories of friends she had met, things she had done, places she visited, and observations of nature, people, and life around her. When I read and re-read her letters, I felt as if she was there, chatting with me. I kept her journals. As I flipped through the pages, trying to find solace in words she had written, I came upon her words of wisdom in the following poem:

> *You ask your ragged heart to keep on beating*
> *You want to sleep without a wakeful edge*
> *You keep on moving,*
> *Trying to stay one step ahead of the shadows that you feel will engulf you,*
> *Trying to stay ahead of nightfall*
> *But perhaps you need to stay still*
> *Let night descend and learn that the sun will rise and dawn will break.*

I was not aware that in Siu-Ling's final days, amid the flutter of friends and family going in and out of our house, Jeff had also been rushed to the hospital because of chest pain. I was busy tending to Siu-Ling's visitors, serving drinks and snacks, running back and forth in a daze, as I tried to cater to our visitors and exchange a few words with everyone. That's just the way we are in our family. Anyone coming for a visit was always offered something to eat or drink. Nobody told me anything when they took Jeff to the hospital. I only found out weeks later. It turns out there was nothing physically wrong with him either, except for the pain of a broken heart. It was extremely stressful for Jeff to deal with what his much-loved sister was going through, watching her life draining away without being able to do anything about it.

How are we supposed to go on living without Siu-Ling? Our hearts were broken, but we had to keep going and be there for each other as we tried to pick up the pieces of our broken hearts.

Siu-Ling was the strong one, the rock in our family, the person we all turned to and leaned on. She was there when there was something I did not understand or when I did not know how to solve a problem, even though I was the mother, the older one who should also have been the wiser one. We often wondered, "What would Siu-Ling have said? What would she have done?"

Friends entrusted Siu-Ling with personal and work problems. She was the one who would counsel and advise them without judgment or give them shelter when they needed a safe place to stay. There's an emptiness in our lives we have to learn to live with. How are we supposed to cope and come to terms with such a loss?

CHAPTER 11

Finding Solace in the Mists of My Grief

Death ends a life but not a relationship.
~Mitch Albom

GRIEF .... What is it? A five-letter word that has a tremendous impact on our lives. It rips us apart and shatters our souls. Grief overwhelms us and affects our physical being, like in the case of broken heart syndrome, as described above. Grief impacts us physically and emotionally. Apart from the intense pain in our hearts, it makes us feel numb, lost, and empty. It can affect our behavior, as when we lash out in anger about the unfairness of life or over feelings of guilt and resentment. Grief can also impact us socially, when we withdraw or isolate ourselves from others and don't care about anything anymore. It plunges us into a cesspool of indescribable pain and sorrow. How are we supposed to carry on?

Grief changes our lives, but it must be acknowledged. It is not something we can just brush off and pretend everything is okay. We must allow ourselves to grieve and express our emotions in a healthy and constructive way. As the saying goes, it is okay to not be okay. It's okay to feel sad, so let grief wash over you, but do not wallow and drown in it. Try to keep your head above it. Knowing that grief and love are tightly intertwined may help you understand the pain of grief. We only grieve for the loss of someone we love.

The University of California's Dual Diagnosis program discusses coping styles and how people react to psychological stress as they try to maintain mental health and emotional well-being. We react differently to different kinds of stress. Life-changing stress like the loss of a loved one, the loss of a job, a divorce, etc. are negative events that require coping skills to adapt and coping strategies to adjust to the negative changes in our lives, as we learn to deal with the pain of our loss and adapt to this change.

As I navigated my grief journey, I read all kinds of books about loss, life and death, the afterlife, and how people dealt with loss. These helped, but I had to find my own way. I participated in a grief workshop at the Ottawa Regional Cancer Foundation (ORCF), where I met a number of ladies who had lost loved ones to cancer. ORCF offered free one-to-one support for caregivers which helped me gain perspective. Patricia Barrett-Robillard, my wonderful cancer coach, helped me through my darkest moments with her kindness, patience, and understanding. Cancer coaches are health professionals (nurses/social workers) with training in oncology and health coaching. In addition, I participated in ORCF's yoga workshop, where I learned how to meditate. I was also able to take advantage of reiki sessions offered by ORCF volunteers. ORCF charged a nominal fee for these sessions, the proceeds of which help the Foundation support cancer patients and their families.

Reiki is an ancient form of energy therapy that involves the transfer of energy that, in my case, released pent-up emotions. There were times when I broke down and cried during my reiki sessions. It did help me feel a bit better each time. Voltaire, one of the greatest of all French writers, said, "Tears are the silent language of grief," and Shakespeare stated, "To weep is to make less the depth of grief."

They say that everything happens for a reason, although I cannot imagine why my daughter had to have cancer and die! Karen Salmansohn, a best-selling self-help book author, wrote, "Often it's the deepest pain which empowers you to grow into your higher self." I had to find out for myself if that was true as I tried to find meaning in the loss of my beloved child. I focused on the things Siu-Ling had accomplished as a daughter, sister, friend, and in her life and work in the Arctic.

My adventurous daughter saw leaving this earth as embarking on a journey to an unknown land to start a new adventure. Her physical absence left a hole in my heart that slowly filled with warm memories of her kindness, thoughtfulness, dedication to her dog team, and work as a wildlife biologist to improve life in Canada's Eastern Arctic. I remembered the love we shared and told myself that it was time to carry on, take care of myself, and be there for the rest of the family. Life goes on. The world does not stop for me or for anyone wallowing in misery. As Siu-Ling so wisely said in her no-nonsense way, *"The world is not fair. The world is not out to get you; the world does not revolve around you. So, get over it."*

As I was going through my grief journey, I discovered that life holds the key to healing. Life is a precious gift. Let's open our eyes and embrace it. We can find healing in life and in things in the world around us that we tend to take for granted. These overlooked parts of life hold the power to heal that helped me find solace in the mists of my grief. I hope they will do the same for you.

The Power of Love

Sophocles once said, "One word frees us of all the weight and pain of life. That word is LOVE." It has been said, time and time again, that love is eternal. Even though our loved one left this earth, our love will never die. Love transcends all dimensions with an invisible bond no one can sever. Our loved ones live on in our hearts and memories forever.

David Kessler, a grief specialist, tells us to give grief some *dedicated time* by remembering the person we lost with more love than pain and by remembering our loved one's life, not their death. Loss is a part of our life, and we naturally feel grief when we lose someone we love. Gordon Wheeler, a clinical psychologist, explains that "grief is the reminder of the depth of our love," and Jann Arden, a Canadian singer and songwriter said, "Grief is the lingering gift of love." May love lighten the darkness of your grief.

The Power of Pets

"My dog is my solace," a friend exclaimed after losing his father. Indeed! Dogs have a way of knowing when you're sad. They provide distraction and help their owners maintain a positive identity and sense of self. I speak for myself when I say that having a dog by my side when I am feeling blue comforts me. Scientific evidence corroborates that a pet helps ease the pain of loneliness, depression, anxiety, and stress. A study by Alan Beck, a psychologist at Purdue University, and psychiatrist Aaron Katcher of the University of Pennsylvania, confirmed the mental health benefits of having a pet. They found that petting and playing with a pet reduces blood pressure, slows down heart rate, and relaxes muscle tension as breathing becomes more regular. Cuddling a cat or dog raises our levels of serotonin and dopamine, the "happiness hormones." A dog does not judge you. When he reaches his paw to you or puts his head on your lap and looks at you with loving eyes, isn't it as if he is saying, "I understand, I am here for you, and I love you with all my heart." Doesn't that help us feel better? Caring for a dog, and taking him out for a walk or run outdoors, preferably in nature, not only tightens our bonds with our furry friends, but also supports our physical health through exercise and self-care.

The Power of Exercise

When Siu-Ling was first diagnosed with cancer, it was a major stressor in my life. I was distraught, confused, and felt at a loss as I tried to cope with the fear of losing my beloved child. I didn't know what to do, but I knew the importance of exercise for staying healthy and relieving stress and anxiety. It also offered a distraction from my negative thoughts. Physical exercise was something I needed, something I had to do. Although the link between depression, anxiety, and exercise isn't entirely clear, research on this topic by the Mayo Clinic shows that the psychological and physical benefits of exercise can help improve mood and ease symptoms of depression or anxiety. Regular physical activity releases endorphins, the feel-good hormone, and other natural brain chemicals that can help you feel better, take your mind off negative thoughts, and make you feel less fretful and fearful.

Exercise in almost any form is good for your body, mental health, mood, and attitude. Being physically active was an important aspect of Siu-Ling's life. While undergoing chemotherapy, she still made an effort to go for a walk with the dogs, every single day. She always managed to find new trails in the area. It was a great comfort for me to be with her as we explored new walking trails. In addition to our daily walks, Siu-Ling went to Liquid Gym, which offers exercise in a pool, with her friend Natalia. She also exercised on the rowing machine in our basement.

One day I received a booklet in the mail which listed recreational programs offered by the city of Ottawa. I saw a program for aquafit classes at the local pool, which piqued my interest. As a child growing up in a hot, tropical country, I used to love swimming and splashing around in water. I did not know much about aquafit, but I figured it would be fun to try. Going for a swim was something I always looked forward to. Exercising with a group of ladies to improve health and well-being was one strategy to keep me occupied and deal with the black cloud hanging over my head after my daughter's cancer diagnosis.

And don't forget dancing; it's a great form or exercise and a great way to express emotion. Certain animals dance, too—for instance, when they are courting or feeling happy. Just google <animals dancing> and watch animals dancing on YouTube. It is funny, and if you get a laugh out of it, that's good, because laughter is the best medicine. Laughter strengthens your immune system and boosts your mood. Dr. Khajuria, a psychiatrist in Los Angeles, wrote, "Increased use of humor in the period following the death of a spouse was found to promote greater emotional resilience." The same holds true after the death of a child or loved one.

The Power of Friendship

It turned out that exercise has other benefits that helped me when times were tough. Joining an aquafit class for seniors gave me the chance to meet and socialize with people in my age group as I tried to deal with the pain in my heart. Instead of wallowing in sorrow, I was doing something to help make myself feel better. It was tough, but I met a group of nice ladies who became my friends. They must have noticed how quiet and withdrawn I was. Besides a smile, I never said much when we were getting dressed after our exercise session. One day, one of the ladies came up to me. She introduced herself and asked how I was. I said I was okay, but I somehow blurted out that my daughter had been diagnosed with cancer. I didn't really know this lady, and I don't know why I told her, but the words just spilled out of my mouth, like a cup that was overflowing. Unlike that nurse in the hospital where I was volunteering who distanced herself from me when I told her about my daughter's cancer, this nice lady embraced me with kindness and compassion. The next time I came to our session, a couple of the ladies handed me cards to express their sympathy. That gesture touched me deeply. Especially when they also gave me a little booklet with poems to lift my spirits. I was most grateful for those little acts of kindness. These senior ladies have lived Life. They knew and understood the ups and downs of Life and tried to make mine a little better. For that I am grateful. Feeling gratitude helped me feel more positive. It also built friendly relations with my newfound friends.

After our exercise session, they asked if I would like to join them at Tim Horton's for coffee and a little treat. Tim Horton was an iconic Canadian ice hockey player and four-time Stanley Cup winner who owned a fast-food franchise of doughnut and coffee shops all across Canada. He sadly died in a traffic accident when he was only 44 years old. Going to Tim's is a Canadian way of saying going for coffee. Although having coffee and a donut meant adding calories to the ones we just burned in class, it was more about camaraderie, togetherness, caring, and sharing a laugh or two. It was balm for my troubled soul.

In addition to my newfound friends, I was grateful for my social circle of old friends I'd had for decades, friends who cared and who I could depend on when I needed someone to talk to. In times like this, we have to reach out for support; social isolation will only make our anxiety and grief worse and can lead to depression. The intense sorrow and pain after we lost Siu-Ling made me withdraw into myself. I did not feel like talking to anybody. I did not feel like seeing anybody, and I did not feel like doing anything. It was as if I had fallen into an abyss, chased by shadows that were about to overwhelm me. It was during that time when a friend called to inquire how I was. I'll never forget what she said. "When you find yourself in a deep, dark valley, you have to keep moving. The mountains are hard to climb. It's going to be tough, but you have to keep going up and up, one step at a time until you see the light, or darkness will swallow you."

Be gentle with yourself. Your loved one would want that for you. Make an effort to interact with others, even if only for a short time. Maybe it's time to revive old friendships, reconnect with good friends you feel comfortable with, even if you may not have seen them or talked to them in a while. This is when you discover who your true friends are. Having such friends is a blessing to be thankful for and should never be taken for granted.

The Power of Creativity

In the meantime, I also decided to do something creative. It is said that creative activity is a powerful therapeutic means to overcome anxiety, loneliness, pain, and sadness. Many artists, musicians, and authors turned the darkest periods in their lives into some of the world's most beautiful works of art, music, and structures through the ages.

Marie Forgeard, of the University of Pennsylvania, conducted research into the relationship between self-reported posttraumatic growth and creativity. Her study suggests that creative individuals may be able to "channel their negative experiences as sources of inspiration and motivation for their work."

Julia Cameron, a teacher, author, poet, playwright, and filmmaker once said, "Creativity – like human life itself – begins in darkness." Creative activity is a powerful therapeutic means to overcome anxiety, loneliness, pain, and sadness.

After having lived in the Netherlands for almost ten years, my thoughts went to Vincent van Gogh (1853-1890), a Dutch post-impressionist painter and one of the greatest artists of all time. Van Gogh was a sensitive soul and suffered a mental breakdown when the girl he fell in love with rejected his marriage proposal. He lacked self-confidence and struggled with his identity. When he moved to Belgium in 1880, he immersed himself in painting but was never known as an artist during his lifetime. The only painting he ever sold during his life was named "Starry Night." It depicts rhythm, beauty, color, and emotion and later became his most famous painting. Van Gogh lived in poverty and suffered from malnutrition. He used the money he received from his brother Theo to buy paint and other art supplies, coffee, and cigarettes. He struggled with depression and mental illness throughout his life and spent a couple of years in an asylum in France. Painting was his solace. It was only after his death that he became known for the beauty and depth of his paintings.

I loved drawing and coloring as a child and, as the days after Siu-Ling's diagnosis went on, I decided to do something creative and take tole painting classes to keep my mind away from negative thoughts and a lingering worry about my daughter's health and well-being.

Tole painting is a decorative art form that started in the 1800s. It uses one-stroke brush techniques to create folk art designs on common household objects. It reminds me of times when people used to create beautiful personal objects for weddings, births, anniversaries, and other special occasions. I loved tole painting and the thought and care that went into each work of art when times were simpler. Making a plain wooden object look pretty gave me a sense of accomplishment, wonder, and satisfaction. I managed to paint a rocking chair and jewelry box for my granddaughter, as well as a mailbox and several gifts I gave to Siu-Ling. Those were personal gifts, gifts from the heart. It made me happy to see how much my family appreciated what, one day, would hopefully become an heirloom that will remind them of how much I love them.

Focusing on the joy of creating things and sharing them with the people I love was a way to channel my negative thoughts and emotions that helped me feel grounded. While I loved to paint, you might want to create a quilt with your loved one in mind, do needlework, cross-stitch, embroidery, knitting, pottery, carving, woodworking, scrapbooking, or whatever strikes your fancy. Anything you can do with your hands that requires concentration can help.

Have you seen adult coloring books? Adult coloring books have been around for decades. *Secret Garden: An Inky Treasure Hunt and Coloring Book* is an adult coloring book that sold millions of copies around the world. So, what is the hype about adult coloring books? When I was on a 7-hour flight from Ottawa to London, I saw a woman engrossed in a coloring book. I was intrigued and wondered how an adult could be so absorbed in what I thought of as a pre-school activity. I remember how my little children used to lie on their tummies on the floor or sit at the kitchen table with frowned foreheads, licking their lips as they intently filled blank spaces with an array of colors to create a picture that they would proudly give to me. Oh, the joy of those precious little gifts! I kept them in a box labeled "Mom's Treasures." Believe it or not, I still have them.

In contrast, adult coloring books are filled with intricate, inspiring patterns and designs that are supposed to provide stress relief and mental relaxation. These books are touted by social media and marketers as therapy for anxiety and stress reduction. Does it work? Some people swear by it. They say that focusing on a fancy black and white pattern and filling it with colors takes their mind away from troubling thoughts and anxieties. Coloring makes a page come alive, and that makes them feel good. Why not get yourself an adult coloring book and a box of colored pencils or markers and see if it works for you? There's no harm in trying, and it does not cost much.

Creativity is not limited to arts and crafts, painting, drawing, and coloring – things you make or do with your hands. Creativity extends to other activities that require time and thought. Composing a song, writing stories, poetry, a diary, you name it, the possibilities are endless.

The Power of Nature

If you like gardening, you may be inspired to putter around in the garden, dig in the soil, and plant flowers that remind you of your loved one. I know of a young woman who created a garden in memory of her mother who was killed in a car accident. She designed a memorial garden in the yard of the local church her mother was actively involved in. Tending that garden gave peace to the daughter and also to the parishioners who knew her mother.

A dear friend of Siu-Ling's planted a tree in her honor and named it the Siu-Ling tree. There are so many ways to help you soothe your aching heart and find peace in nature. I love going for a walk wherever I can. It helps me calm down and recharge myself. Depending on where you live, you may be able to spend time in your garden, a community garden, a city park, playgrounds, forests, the beach, a lake, meadow, mountains, a campground, or wherever you find nature nearby. I am sure you'll find someplace that will feel right to you. Here's a practice you can try when you're out in nature:

- *Find somewhere quiet to sit*
- *Shake your arms to loosen up*
- *Gently turn your head from side to side a couple of times*
- *Close your eyes*

- *Take a couple of deep breaths*
- *Listen to the sounds around you and focus on them.*
- *What do you hear? Maybe birds twittering in treetops? The whisper of a gentle breeze, the voices of little children in the background?*
- *Find gratitude for that moment as you connect with your loved one in your mind and focus on the happy times and moments that bring a smile to your face.*

Life goes on. Days come and go. The world is alive, and so are we. Let's pull ourselves together and make a conscious decision to get out of this rut and move on. We can do it, one little step at a time. That does not mean that we'll forget our loved ones, for they will always be in our hearts, no matter where we are. In time, we'll learn to adapt to the new normal. Siu-Ling said, "Only you can choose how you will react." David Kessler said it beautifully when he wrote, "A part of the old you died with your loved one, but a part of your loved one lives in the new you."

The Power of Music

Why not listen to music? Music is a powerful tool that helped me feel better during my grief journey. The song "You'll never walk alone" by Richard Rogers gives me chills, uplifts my spirit, and, sometimes, brings tears to my eyes, depending on my mood.

Victor Hugo, one of the greatest and best-known French writers, said, "Music expresses that which cannot be put into words and that which cannot remain silent." Music is an integral part of our lives from the time we first heard our mothers sing us lullabies when we were babies. Regardless of our cultural background, who or where we are, or what stage of life we are in, music touches us in many ways.

Music describes feelings of happiness, pain, sadness, longing, and loneliness. Life would be dull without the sound of music, the sound of voices and musical instruments, or the sound of birds singing in the treetops. Please, take a quiet moment and think about it. How does music make you feel? Have you ever swayed, danced, hopped, hummed, or tapped your feet to the sound of music?

Listening to happy classical music gives me feelings of peace and calm. If you like classical music, do a web search for < happy classical music >, and you'll find uplifting, inspiring, and motivational pieces of music by Vivaldi, Mozart, Beethoven, Strauss, and others that nurture your spirit and give you moments of peace and quiet. I also like listening to German Oktoberfest and beer-drinking songs that make me want to jump up, dance, and sway to the music. It reminds me of our happy times in Germany during Oktoberfest, gathering with friends to laugh, sing, clap, sway, and merrily shout to beer-drinking songs. I remember the infectious, carefree, happy, and jolly atmosphere of Oktoberfest in Munich, a city we had a special connection to, as Bing and I spent the first years of our married life there. Munich is the city where Siu-Ling was born. Munich, therefore, has a special place in our hearts. It was my home away from home. The Bavarian family who shared their home with us not only welcomed us into their home, they also welcomed us into their hearts.

Our landlady, Frau Loebmann, reminded me of Mrs. Claus. She was a jolly, big-bosomed old lady with round rosy cheeks, bright blue eyes, and silvery-grey hair tied in a bun on top of her head. She always wore a starched white apron around the house. Her husband, Herr

Dr. Loebmann, always referred to his wife as *Mutti* (mother) when he spoke to us. "Is *Mutti* home? Have you seen *Mutti*?" and, before long, Frau Loebmann became *Mutti* to me.

The Loebmanns treated us like family. *Mutti* and I often stood side by side in the kitchen while she prepared her Sunday *Schweinebraten* (roast pork), and I made *hutspot*, a Dutch stew made of potatoes, onions, carrots, and corned beef. After dinner, *Mutti* often invited us into their cozy *Stube* (parlor) with its traditional tiled stove to watch television and share a glass of wine. We enjoyed listening to classical music and watching operettas together, a form of theatre that includes spoken dialogue, songs, and dance. Our appreciation and love for German music and culture created a bond with this Bavarian family, and Bavaria became a second home to me.

Music isn't just a form of art or entertainment but a way to bring people together. It can cheer you up, comfort you, but also stir, thrill, and excite you. Doesn't the sight of little children wiggling, dancing or happily jumping up and down to the sound and rhythm of music bring a smile to your face? Music also expresses feelings of fear, anger, hopelessness, aggression, and despair, like in the case of Ludwig von Beethoven, one of the greatest musicians of all time. When Beethoven started losing his hearing, he wrote his Fifth Symphony, which later became known as the "Symphony of Fate." He found his increasing deafness difficult to deal with and sank into a deep depression. In the *Heiligenstadt Testament*, a letter he wrote to his brothers, he described his frustrations, pain, and suffering about the loss of his hearing, his growing isolation, and his thoughts of suicide. However, it was his commitment to music that ultimately saved him. The first four notes in the opening motif of his Fifth Symphony depict his struggle with

Fate and later became known the world over as a powerful symbol for the Allied forces.

Bob Marley, reggae's most transcendent and iconic figure, once said, "One thing about music, when it hits you, you feel no pain." His songs of faith, devotion, and revolution created a legacy that continues to live on through his music and lyrics about heartbreak, suffering, tears, pain, and loss. Marley suffered his share of pain, especially from the time he was diagnosed with malignant melanoma at the height of his career when he was 32 years old until his death at 36 in 1981.

In "The Life and Times of Bob Marley," Mikal Gilmore wrote, "Bob Marley was already dying when he stood on stage in Pittsburgh that night in September 1980." In spite of what limited time the singer had left on earth, he continued writing, recording, and going on exhaustive tours that took a heavy toll on him.

During a concert at Madison Square Garden on September 20, 1980, Marley almost passed out during his performance. When he woke up the following day, Marley was confused and unable to remember what had happened the night before. Later, while jogging with a friend in Central Park, he suddenly collapsed. A visit to the doctor confirmed what he had been dreading. According to Gilmore, Marley's blackout had been due to a brain tumor. Cancer had spread to his lungs, liver, and brain and was terminal. At that point, he probably only had a couple of weeks to live. As Marley neared the end, he was totally drained and cried out for God to take him. His wife, Rita, wrote that she held him in her arms and sang to him until he started weeping. That's when he told her with whatever strength he had left in his voice, "Don't cry. Keep on singing."

Music is a powerful tool. Music has always been important to our family, especially to Siu-Ling—in good times and in bad times. I was not aware that Siu-Ling started writing songs when she was in high school. She kept it to herself until her musician friend, Rob, discovered it and convinced her to share it with the world. I am glad he did.

If you play a musical instrument, why don't you pick it up and start playing? If you don't play a musical instrument, you can hum or sing - even if it's only in the shower. It helps take your mind off negative thoughts and helps you feel a little better.

The Power of Words

In an article that appeared in the *HuffPost*, Dr. Hyder Zahed emphasized, "Words are singularly the most powerful force available to humanity. We can choose to use this force constructively with words of encouragement or destructively using words of despair. Words have energy and power with the ability to help, to heal, to hinder, to hurt, to harm, to humiliate and to humble."

Yes, words have the energy and power to help and heal. Putting words to paper, like in journaling, is another creative way to express the kind of feelings that you might not be able to share with anyone but yourself. Write a letter to your loved one as if they were still alive and store it in a special box. Write notes, a poem, a story. Get yourself a nice journal or a simple exercise book, the kind kids get in school. Write whatever comes to mind, whatever you feel, without inhibitions, as if you were writing a letter to a trusted, nonjudgmental friend. Let it all out. It will help make you feel better.

According to an article in the *New York Times*, "Journaling is one of the more effective acts of self-care. It also is one of the cheapest."

Scientific studies have shown that journaling boosts mindfulness, memory, and communication skills." Dr. James J. Pennebaker, a pioneer of writing therapy, is a social psychologist at the University of Texas, Austin. He wrote, "Journaling about traumatic or disturbing experiences specifically has the most measurable impact on our overall well-being." Writing down negative feelings like sadness, anger, pain, frustration, or grief in a journal helps you to *brain dump*, a term Dr. Pennebaker uses to describe relieving the tension that prevents you from feeling happy.

David Kessler, one of the most well-known experts and lecturers on death and grieving, said that writing is a dynamic tool for healing in our busy lives. It is important to take the time to reflect and listen to your spirit. Our stories must be shared and our grief must be witnessed. I believe that grief is something that must be acknowledged and not brushed away, for without grief, there is no love. Do we grieve when we read that someone we never heard of or do not know has died? It is sad, but no, it does not affect us. Does it leave a hole in our hearts? No! We may feel sorry, but it does not compare to the pain of losing someone near and dear to you. Nobody knows and understands the indescribable emptiness and unbearable pain of such a loss unless they have experienced it themselves.

In his book, *Finding Meaning: The Sixth Stage of Grief*, Kessler writes that "grief may not end but it can change shape and be a source of generosity, love and meaning. An essential component of living with grief is the ability to construct meaning out of tragedy." He said, "Finding meaning in loss empowers us to find a path forward. Meaning helps us make sense of grief."

Writing my book about Siu-Ling's life in Iqaluit and her dog team during the last years of her life, when she was still by my side, taught me not only about Siu-Ling and her love for nature, the Arctic, its people, and wildlife, but also about the history of her amazing dogs. Focusing on my writing helped me deal with the difficult times after her diagnosis and my fear of losing her. And when I lost her, I had to find meaning in the kind of loss no words can describe. I am slowly starting to see through the mists of my grief like Siu-Ling did when she lost her much-loved furry friend, Rupert, who meant the world to her. She wrote an ode to Rupert that could apply to anyone's loss of a loved one:

Oh, I will carry you into my dreams
Let memories wash over me like a stream
And I will need you with my every breath,
Feel you beside me with my every step
What the senses remember
The heart never forgets
And the dark of December
Will be lit by a love that burns yet,
The patient joy of the love that we share.
Though you may go, in my heart, it will always be there
So, go ahead, it's alright, it's okay
You'll take the lead but I know when you get there, you'll wait
I know you watch over me as I sleep
And catch my tears when I weep
You've been my love, been my soul, been my friend
And we may part but I know we will be together again

Words are not only to be written. Words are also to be read. Reading is said to positively enhance your life. When times were tough, I tried to read as much as I could to focus my attention on something other than my broken heart. I read a lot of books about spirituality and wanted to know the meaning of life, but that is a question I still have not found an answer to. I wanted to find out if there was a connection between the here and now, the past, and the future. I wondered about my connection with the world around me. I read about psychics and mediums and questioned if they could really communicate with spirits. I also wondered how you can tell the real ones from the fake ones. But I also read novels, magazines, poetry, and inspiring quotes about love and life by famous people.

You may find comfort in reading the Bible, Qur'an, or any book or magazine that grabs your interest. It is up to you. Try it. Getting immersed in a book passes time, keeps your mind engaged, and is said to benefit both physical and mental health.

A study about health and blood pressure on *Healthline*, an online resource covering all facets of physical and mental health, found that "thirty minutes of reading lowered blood pressure, heart rate, and feelings of psychological distress, just as effectively as yoga and humor did." It also shows that regular reading fights depression symptoms, reduces stress, and aids in sleep readiness. It certainly is worth a try. While we who have lost our loved ones will never get over our loss, the fact that they are physically absent is something we will have to learn to live with, we'll always remember the things we used to do together, the memories we created, and the love we shared. When those memories start bringing a smile to our face, instead of just tears, we *can* transform the pain of loss into something to honor our loved ones and keep their spirits alive. We can do that by doing good and making this world a little better.

Finding Meaning in our Loss

So, as you can see from some of the thoughts I've shared here, there are many ways to at least ease the ragged edges of your broken heart and, hopefully, help you heal. I have only shared the ones that I used on my journey. The important thing to remember is that you should find something to help mend your broken heart that resonates with you and helps you stay connected to life, living, the world, and the people around you. Grief may not end but, I believe, it can change shape and, as David Kessler said, "be a source of generosity, love and meaning." He added that, "An essential component of living with grief is the ability to construct meaning out of tragedy." The Dalai Lama said, "The way through the sadness and grief that comes from great loss is to use it as motivation, and to generate a deeper sense of purpose." Many people have created memorials to preserve the memory of a loved one. Some examples are as simple as planting a tree or garden or dedicating a bench in a park in memory of a loved one, like a good friend of mine did after his wife passed away.

In May 2013, Rowan Stringer, a 17-year-old Ottawa student who was captain of her school's rugby team, suffered a severe concussion and fatal blow to her head during a game. Her death led to new concussion safety legislation in Ontario. It was named *Rowan's Law* in her honor to increase awareness about concussion in sports and Ontario's plan to improve concussion safety.

David Pelly and his wife Laurie established the *Ayalik Fund* in 2015 in honor of their beloved son, Eric Ayalik Okalitana Pelly, a little Inuk boy they fostered, then adopted when he was a toddler. Eric died unexpectedly at home, while asleep, of sudden cardiac arrhythmia. The *Ayalik Fund* aims to give Inuit youth who are born into difficult circumstances a boost as they navigate modern adolescence in the challenging environment of the North. The Pellys believe that if youth are provided adequate support and guidance during these critical developmental years, they have a much greater likelihood of growing their self-esteem and confidence, learning how to set and achieve personal goals, and flourishing.

May these ideas I shared here provide you with inspiration to keep you going through your grief journey and help you find solace and peace.

CHAPTER 12

Love Never Dies

When someone is in your heart, they're never really gone.
They can come back to you, even at unlikely times.
~Mitch Albom

As we prepared for our first Christmas without our beloved Siu-Ling, we remembered the 52 Christmases we had with her. Siu-Ling always made an effort to be with us every single Christmas of her life, regardless of the distance between us. Even when we lived in the Netherlands from 1989 until 1999, Siu-Ling would jump on a plane to spend the Christmas holidays with us in Europe. It is something to be thankful for. Christmas 2016 would have been our 53rd Christmas with Siu-Ling. Instead, it became our first Christmas without her. There was an emptiness not only in my heart but in everyone's in the family. I was just going through the motions when I was decorating our Christmas tree. I did not feel the usual excitement of unpacking each ornament that I had carefully packed away when I took the Christmas tree down the day after Epiphany—when Siu-Ling was still with us.

Each ornament evoked a memory of love, life, fun, and family that represented part of our *love tree*: the colorful felt ornaments I made with our kids, the delicate, antique glass balls from my childhood that reflected our Christmas tree lights, and the tiny handmade wooden ornaments I bought at Christmas markets in Germany. When it was time to hang the family's Christmas stockings on the mantelpiece, I was alone in the family room. I picked up Siu-Ling's stocking, held it in front of me, and clutched it to my heart as I started bawling my head off. Lillian, Siu-Ling's retired sled dog, who lived with us, came to me, looked at me with her dewy almond eyes, and put her chin on my lap. She knew I needed her. I stroked her soft, silky head, dug my fingers in the thick fur around her neck, and tickled her behind her ears. She liked that. I got up and hung Siu-Ling's stocking on the mantelpiece where it belonged. I wrote her a note to tell her how much I loved her and stuck it in her stocking.

Life does not stand still. I had to hang in and move along, or I knew I would sink into despair, wandering around a barren wasteland with nowhere to go. I could not let that happen. Siu-Ling would not want me to. I had a family to think of, a family I loved and who loved me. I had a choice, a choice of how to react. There are things in life one cannot change, but we can learn to adapt. Things will never be the same, but we can overcome, one step at a time. We have to.

They say that believing in life after death when we are grieving helps comfort us, and that when our loved one is gone, she remains with us in spirit. They say that love never dies and that our connection with our lost loved one does not end. Even though Siu-Ling is not physically present, I'd like to believe that she is still around. When I mourn the loss of my beloved child, I try to find solace in art, music, songs, and poetry, even though the comfort of these things will be laced with tears. But as time goes by, the tears will lessen. The pain won't be as intense when we shift our focus to sweet memories of love and life instead of sickness and death.

Siu-Ling must have known she was dying when she wrote *I Am With You Everywhere*. She must have believed that, although she would no longer be on earth in her physical form, she would still be with us and *shine like the diamonds in the snow*. She wanted us to feel her *warmth in the sunrise casting gold*, and see *the brightness that flames in autumn leaves*, as she *whispers like the wind among the pines and sings in the mountains high and free*. Everywhere she is, everywhere we'll be, we'll always be together. Yes, we will.

Gone From My Sight, a poem that was presumably written by the Rev. Luther F. Beecher (1813–1903) and often attributed to Henry van Dyke (1852 – 1933), is a metaphor about dying that has given me solace:

Gone From My Sight

I am standing upon the seashore.
A ship at my side spreads her white sails to the
moving breeze and starts for the blue ocean.
She is an object of beauty and strength.
I stand and watch her until, at length, she hangs
like a speck of white cloud, just where the sea and sky
come to mingle with each other.

Then, someone at my side says, "There, she is gone."

Gone where?

Gone from my sight. That is all.
She is just as large in mast, hull,
and spar as she was when she left my side.
And, she is just as able to bear her load of
living freight to her destined port.
Her diminished size is in me—not in her.

And, just at the moment when someone says,
"There, she is gone," there are other eyes watching her
coming, and other voices ready to take up the glad shout,
"Here she comes!"

And that is dying.

Before Siu-Ling passed away, she said she was not afraid of dying. I *have to* believe that everywhere she is, everywhere we are, we'll always be together, even though we can't see her.

One snowy evening, I went for a walk with Lillian, who had become my loyal, furry companion. Siu-Ling and I used to always rejoice in the uninhibited joyfulness of her dogs as they ran ahead, happy and free in wide-open spaces, enjoying every moment of being. As I walked down the street with Lillian by my side that evening, this sedate eleven-year-old dog suddenly took off like the wind and started digging her nose and paws in the snow. She must have caught the scent of a rabbit, of which there are a few in our neighborhood. I was delighted to see that she still had it in her to run that fast when, out of the blue, I realized that Siu-Ling wasn't there to share that moment with me. Hot tears streamed down my cheeks as I trudged home in the evening gloom. Except for the sound of my boots crunching the snow, it was very quiet. The street was deserted. I stopped under a streetlight and looked up at the darkened sky, yearning for a glimpse of my lovely daughter. A shower of snow crystals glittering in the streetlight's glow drifted down on me, cooling my face, when Lillian trotted to my side and rubbed herself affectionately against my leg. I'd like to believe it was a message from Siu-Ling telling me not to be sad. I know she'll *watch over me as I sleep and catch my tears when I weep* (from Siu-Ling's *Ode to Rupert*). I try to find comfort in little things that I believe might be messages from her, like the day I was standing in the kitchen and was so upset about something that I cried out for her. Suddenly, a tiny yellow bird I had never seen before appeared and hopped onto a pot of flowers I had on the deck outside my kitchen. It stayed for a couple of seconds, twittering before it flew away. Those couple of seconds were enough to distract me and take my mind off my distress as I stood in wonder, admiring the beauty of this tiny yellow warbler. Warblers are said to symbolize joy and a positive outlook on life. They show up as a spirit guide when you need guidance or direction.

One day I was sitting at my kitchen table and talking to Lynn, Siu-Ling's friend who had become part of our family, when a blue jay accidentally flew against my window and then perched, a little dazed from the impact, on the deck railing. It stayed there long enough for me to admire its pointed crest, its beautiful bright blue color, and the white tips of its wings. A blue jay is said to symbolize long-lasting friendships and relationships. It so happened that a blue jay is also the symbol of the high school Siu-Ling attended.

The day she was cremated, Jeff and his family were sitting out on the deck when a hummingbird appeared and hovered over them. The next day, Diane, Jeff's wife, was standing by the sink in front of their kitchen window when she saw a hummingbird hovering over their two sled dogs, Frances and Nunu, that were tied up in their backyard. Frances and Nunu are Inuit Dogs Siu-Ling gave Jeff when they were puppies. Was Siu-Ling checking in on them and letting Diane know she was near?

There was something about hummingbirds that somehow seemed connected to Siu-Ling. The day the vet came to the house to put Siu-Ling's furry friend, Rupert, down as he was dying of cancer, a hummingbird hovered in front of the living room window during the procedure. That summer, our family went camping in Nova Scotia. Rupert had been a big part of the family and always came with us. It was our first camping trip without Rupert. We set up camp on Graves Island Provincial Park, an oceanside campground on Nova Scotia's south shore where we camped every August. Suddenly, a hummingbird appeared out of nowhere and perched on the branch of a tall dead tree overlooking our site, as if it was checking on us. It was strange, for there was nothing in the area that would have attracted a hummingbird. When we moved to our next campground in Cape Breton on Nova Scotia's east coast, we had several more visits from hummingbirds. It made me wonder if there was a connection between this tiny flyer and Siu-Ling.

Hummingbirds are considered spiritual messengers. Sue Simm, one of Siu-Ling's closest friends who came to stay with us and took care of us during Siu-Ling's last weeks at home, told me that she had several visits from a hummingbird after Siu-Ling's passing.

Sheila Watt-Cloutier, an Inuk activist and Nobel Peace Prize nominee for her environmental work, happened to be in New Zealand to promote her book *The Right to be Cold* when Siu-Ling passed. She sent me a lovely note in which she wrote that she sensed Siu-Ling's passing. Sheila or *Siila*, her Inuit name, gave me permission to share her message with you.

I sensed Siu-Ling's farewell from all the way here because where she is now where there is no distance to anywhere, and as I said to her when I visited, she would be going to a place where all things are known and where all things are understood.

I absolutely love your story about hummingbirds and the connection to Siu-Ling's ongoing spirit. Because that is what this is. She is letting you know that she is very much present in your lives and that all is well where she is. Just after my mother Daisy died, I saw daisies in all forms everywhere I went. Even in Siberia! She let me know that she was not far away, and that lasted for a few years until I was able to let her go. I saw daisies in true flower form, in magazines, in art, in song, in a dog named Daisy, you name it. Daisies were in my life in many numbers at every turn.

So, for me, your stories about hummingbirds are not strange at all. It is very normal, surreal, and real. It is on the level of spirit and spirituality, and Siu-Ling is making herself known that her spirit lives on. So dear Kim, I also have a story for you which I believe can help you to believe what I say about the work of spirit.

I was in Christchurch, New Zealand, and stayed at a lovely bed and breakfast. Just a block from the B & B, I would go and eat at this little restaurant called Fiddlesticks. The food was pricey but very good, and it was practical to go there often as it was so close by the B & B. On my first meal there, I ordered a decaffeinated cappuccino, and it was the best tasting cappuccino I have ever had. I am not a regular coffee drinker and only have the odd decaffeinated coffee and drink mostly herbal teas. Well, I fell in love with this decaf coffee this little place had and asked if there is a place I may be able to buy the beans and bring them back to Canada with me. Yes, was the answer, and she said I could find them at a grocery store anywhere and that they were high-quality organic beans. I asked what the name was so I could go and look for them. Two days later, someone drove me to the actual store where they roast them, and I bought 5 vacuum-packed bags to bring home. So since leaving Christchurch, NZ, I have had them in my luggage and get a whiff of their wonderful aroma each time I open my bag. So .... the name of the company and the coffee: Hummingbird! How precious is that as a strong message that your dear daughter lives on in spirit and letting us know this. Trust that, dear Kim. These signs are not all coincidences. She is not far from you and your family, and she is letting you all know that. The Hummingbird coffee is so I could reassure you of that.

Wasn't it surreal for Siila to sense Siu-Ling's passing from down under, on the other side of the world? Inuit have a spiritual connection with the land and nature. Inuit spirituality is part of a living, oral tradition. Receiving Siila's heartwarming letter was a great comfort to me. *Nakurmiik* (thank you in Inuktitut), Siila.

A couple of months after Siu-Ling's passing, Jeff had a very vivid dream about her. He told me what he dreamt:

She came to the door and looked in through the window. She lifted the door from its frame and came inside. Looked good, business-like, black jacket and skirt. Was taller than me. Big smile. Me and Kina were there. Kina was squealing, Er! Er! I asked her jokingly if she brought snacks. She was glowing. She came into the house, and I looked at her back, checking for wings. Two spots about 8" long by 2" wide verticals were glowing on her back. She hugged Kina and told her how proud she was of her. She told us she could see us and knew what we were doing and how we were. We walked into the bedroom where Tiny (pet name for Jeff's wife, Diane) was. She hugged Tiny, who was crying. I woke up.

The day Siu-Ling embarked on her adventure into the great beyond, I sat at her bedside as she lay under a beautiful quilt her friend Leanne had sent her. She lay there so still, quiet, and peaceful. I stroked her hair and kissed her face. My heart was aching and felt heavy. I told her how much I loved her and cried my heart out when the room suddenly filled with a light so bright it made me stop and blink. It was as if the sun had burst into the room. At that moment, my 10-year-old grandson, Jin, unexpectedly walked into the room. He put his arms around me and hugged me real tight. My dear little boy, so loving, so sweet and sensitive, there to comfort me in my sorrow.

And so I cope from day to day, as I try to find solace in the mists of my grief. I've tried to find comfort in heartwarming memories and mystifying incidents that seem like messages from Siu-Ling. They have given me the strength to change my attitude about the loss of my beloved child. Now I understand why I did not die when my heart stopped beating. I had to be there for Siu-Ling when her job on earth was done. Siu-Ling's passing was not something I had any control over. It was the nature of things. I just had to be there for her. One thing I do have control over is carrying her close to my heart for as long as I live. My love for my darling daughter spans all dimensions. Love never dies. In spite of her physical absence, love binds us and keeps us together. By honoring Siu-Ling and celebrating her life and the way she tried to make this world a better place, I will uphold her legacy and keep her spirit alive for as long as I can. I will try to

Siu-Ling and her dog team traveling toward the sunset.
(Photo credit: Thomas Godfrey)

make this world a little better, the way she did, through kindness, caring and sharing, compassion, empathy, and understanding. Even though her life on earth was cut short, it was not lived in vain. I am remembering and honoring my daughter by donating all proceeds from the sale of my books to Ilisaqsivik Society's Qimmivut and Wounded Warriors program to support Inuit mental health issues suffered through emotional trauma. I have also established a scholarship for an Inuk student studying Environmental Technology at Nunavut's Arctic college in Iqaluit. This will help young Inuit carry on Siu-Ling's work in wildlife research and management in the North and honor her and her respect and love for its people, environment, and wildlife.

ACKNOWLEDGMENTS

First and foremost, I must thank Siu-Ling for being an inspiration and an integral part of our family. Although my beloved Siu-Ling no longer is with us in physical form, her spirit lingers on. Memories of the love and joy we shared, her words of wisdom, and her quirky sense of humor help us find solace as we learn to live with our grief. My dear child, although your time with us was much too brief, we are thankful that you came into our lives. You left a beautiful imprint in our hearts that will always be there. Thank you for your kind and loving ways, for enriching our family, and for everything you have done to make this world a little better.

My sincere gratitude goes to my friends for their love, kindness, and empathy, especially Brigitta Fernandez, Ursula Mount, Ulla Riester, Ulrike Sati, my neighbor, Doralene Berg. I am also deeply grateful to Siu-Ling's many friends who reached out to me, took me out for walks, invited me and the family for meals, and shared their love and memories of Siu-Ling with me: Robert Aubé, Cory Bell, Amy Caughey, Paul Crowley, Susanne Emond, Shari Fox, Jane George, Thomas Godfrey, Susan and Mark Hamilton, Shannon Hessian, John Kim, Pierre Lecomte, Elise Maltinsky, Debbie McAllister, Matty

McNair, Lynn Peplinski, Janet Pitsiulaaq Brewster, Brigid Rowan, Natalia Rybczynski, Susan Simm, and Emily Woods. Thank you for being there. To Amy and Shannon, and all who helped them organize Siu-Ling's "After Party," a celebration of Siu-Ling's life, thank you for organizing it. Janet, thank you for lighting and tending the *qulliq* (a traditional Inuit lamp that provides light and warmth. It is made of hollowed-out stone and uses the oil of seal or whale blubber for fuel and arctic cotton for a wick) during the celebration. Rob and your band, thank you for the music.

Chris Rogers and Bonnie, thank you for opening your house to host Siu-Ling's friends who had traveled to Ottawa from all over Canada, Great Britain, the United States, the Netherlands, and France to say goodbye.

Patricia Barret-Robillard, my counselor at The Ottawa Regional Cancer Foundation, thank you for being there for me and for your kind and professional guidance. It meant a lot to me.

My love and appreciation to cousins Suzanna Sie and Andy Oey from Holland who supported us during the most challenging time of our lives. Losing Andy, a healthy, strong, and athletic young man, to COVID on Easter Sunday, 2020, when he was only 56 years old, was a big, unexpected blow that added greatly to our sorrow.

Wendy Parker, Siu-Ling's long-time massage therapist, thank you for being there for Siu-Ling when she needed your gentle, soothing touch. Thank you also for your kind, loving, and gentle care. I know how much Siu-Ling appreciated it.

David Stone, Siu-Ling's boss at the Department of Indian and Northern Development, thank you for sharing your memories of Siu-Ling's work on the international protocol of POPs (Persistent

Organic Pollutants) and the NCP (Northern Contaminants Program) management team. It warmed my heart to learn of Siu-Ling's involvement in the assessment of Inuit human health effects resulting from exposure to POPs.

Bruce MacDonald, Siu-Ling's boss at Environment and Climate Change Canada, thank you so much for your touching letter and explanation of Siu-Ling's work and the lasting impact she left on wildlife management in Canada's North.

A great, big thanks to Siu-Ling's dog teaming friends. They took our family and friends on a memorable dog-sledding trip to Qaummaaviit Territorial Park outside Iqaluit, one of Siu-Ling's favorite dogsledding destinations, to celebrate Siu-Ling's life and love for the Arctic and the amazing Canadian Inuit Dog. Five dog teams driven by David Abernathy, Sarah McNair-Landry, Matty McNair, Andrew Maher, and Shannon Hessian with more than 40 of their magnificent Canadian Inuit Dogs ran across the sea ice to the park, after which we all gathered on a ridge, raised our hands with cups of wine, and called out a toast to Siu-Ling that was carried away by the wind. Thank you all for this unforgettable experience to honor Siu-Ling. It touched our very souls. To Meeka Mike, thank you for building the igloo on that ridge that allowed our grandchildren to see, touch, and crawl into its cozy interior and feel what it's like to be in a real igloo.

Robert Aubé, Pierre Lecomte, and Jeff Maurice, thank you for capturing and preserving Siu-Ling's voice and beautiful music on the CD you produced. Thank you for the time, effort, and loving friendship you devoted to it. Thanks also to all the band members who contributed to Siu-Ling's CD: Jamal Shirley, Steve Rigby, Emily Woods, Gina Burgess, and Nancy Mike.

Thank you, Rob, Pierre, Emily, Errol and Paula Fletcher for that last musical session with Siu-Ling in our home three weeks before Siu-Ling passed away. When Siu-Ling picked up the guitar one last time and opened her heart when she started singing *I Am with You Everywhere*, accompanied by Rob and Pierre, as a final goodbye, it was such an emotional but beautiful conclusion to a memorable day. That moment filled my heart with gratitude for the love and friendship you all have for our precious Siu-Ling.

To Susanne Emond, who created that beautiful album with memories from Siu-Ling's friends, thank you from the bottom of my heart. And thank you to all Siu-Ling's friends and colleagues who came from far and wide to see her and show her how much they cared about her.

An extra thank you to friends, family, and colleagues for taking the time to review my manuscript and fill in the blanks, despite their busy schedules: my son Jeff and dear daughter-in-law, Diane; Siu-Ling's friends, Madeleine Cole, Debbie McAllister, Susan Simm, and Natalia Rybczinski; my friend, Susan Hamilton; Pam Culley McCullough, Kymn Harvin, Leslie Bridger, Michael Overlie, Linda Bryce, and Rev. Cathy Silva of the Get Your Book Done Community; Patricia Barrett-Robillard, my cancer coach, and Leahanne Prolas. To Jane George and my old friend and colleague, Madeleine McDonald, and to David Pelly, whom I have not met in person but greatly admire – you all understand the pain and sorrow of losing a child. Thank you all for reviewing my manuscript and your much-appreciated feedback.

A special thank you also to my editor, Susan Bruck, for your understanding, compassion, and meticulous care in going over my manuscript. Having you by my side when I was unsure about a word or phrase was a great help. Ranilo Cabo thank you so much for designing the beautiful, thought-provoking covers that allowed me to choose an image that touched my soul.

This book would not have been possible without Christine Kloser and her amazing team at Capucia Publishing who gave their ongoing guidance, support, and consideration in realizing the birth of my book. My sincere appreciation goes to Jean Merrill and Carrie Jareed for keeping me on my toes. Thank you for your kindness and understanding when times were tough during my writing journey and when I was hopelessly stuck and did not know how to proceed.

I must not forget my family. My special thanks and love go to my husband Bing, sons Jeff and Tim, Jeff's wife Diane, and my grandchildren Kina, Yi Zhen, and Jin for their love, care, and support. You mean the world to me.

Lillian, my sweet furry friend and companion, you were there for me when I needed your loving and comforting presence and nuzzles. It was a privilege to have had you in my life.

Last but not least, thank you to all my readers for acquiring this book. I hope it will offer you some solace in the mists of your grief.

NOTES AND RESOURCES

Chapter 1

1. Randy Pausch (1960-2008) was a professor at the University of Pittsburgh who died of pancreatic cancer when he was only 47 years old. He became a symbol of the beauty and briefness of life when he gave his inspiring "Last Lecture," which has been published as a book.

Chapter 2

1. *The Act of Killing* is an Oscar-nominated documentary by Joshua Oppenheimer about the horrifying mass executions of accused communists in Indonesia from 1965-66.
2. Meister Eckhart (c 1260 – c 1328). German theologian, philosopher, and mystic.
3. William A. Feather (1889-1981). American author and publisher based in Cleveland.

Chapter 3

1. McIntosh, Andrew. "October Crisis." In: *Canadian Encyclopedia*. August 13, 2013: https://www.thecanadianencyclopedia.ca/en/article/october-crisis

2. Government of Canada. "Northern Contaminants Program - Background." https://science.gc.ca/eic/site/063.nsf/eng/h_67223C7F.html

3. Stone, David. "The Changing Arctic Environment: The Arctic Messenger." Cambridge University Press, New York, NY. 2015

4. Government of Canada, Northern Contaminants program. https://science.gc.ca/eic/site/063.nsf/eng/h_7A463DBA.html

Chapter 4

1. Joshua J. Marine is an author who is known for the quote at the beginning of this chapter.

2. Brucks, J.A. "Ovarian cancer. The most lethal gynecologic malignancy." In: *The Nursing Clinics of North America*. 1992. Dec; 27(4): 835-45.

3. Eldridge, Lynne MD, "How anticipatory grief differs from grief after death." In: *Verywell Health*, November 19, 2019. https://www.verywellhealth.com/understanding-anticipatory-grief-and-symptoms-2248855

4. Orloff, Judith. "The Health Benefit of Tears." In: *Psychology Today*. July 27, 2010. https://www.psychologytoday.com/ca/blog/emotional-freedom/201007/the-health-benefits-tears

5. May, Gerald G. "The Wisdom of the Wilderness." Harper Collins, N.Y. 2000.

Chapter 5

1. Han, Kim. *The Canadian Inuit Dog: Icon of Canada's North*. Revodana Publishing, 2018.

2. The Qimualaniq Quest is a 200-mile (320 km) dog sledding race from Iqaluit to Kimmirut and back. Kimmirut is a hamlet on Baffin Island's southwest coast. The race was organized by Nunavut's Francophone Association and Kimmirut's Mayukalik Hunters and Trappers Association to revitalize dog sledding with traditional Inuit Dogs on Baffin Island. The Qimualaniq Quest was considered an opportunity for Inuit, French, and English Canadians living in the North to get together and celebrate living in the Arctic.

   Participants had to carry two 40-kilogram bags (totaling 80 kg/176 pounds) of flour on their *qamutiik* (sled) to recall the olden days when dog teams carried all supplies and game when Inuit went hunting. In addition to the flour, which was used in a feast to welcome the *qimuksiktiit* (dog-teamers), each participant also had to carry a sleeping bag and tent and enough supplies to last at least two days.

3. **Hummock**: "a smooth hill of ice that forms on the sea ice surface from eroding ridges, particularly during the summer melt; the formation of hummocks is similar to young mountain peaks with steep slopes that erode into smooth, rolling hills." https://nsidc.org/cryosphere/glossary?keys=hummock

4. **Pressure ridge**: "a ridge produced on floating ice by buckling or crushing under lateral pressure of wind or tide" (Merriam-Webster).

   When wind, ocean currents, and other forces push sea ice around into piles that rise and form small mountains above the level sea ice surface; ridges are initially thin and transparent with very sharp edges from blocks of ice piling up: https://nsidc.org/cryosphere/glossary?keys=&page=20

I AM WITH YOU EVERYWHERE

5. **Leads** are "narrow, linear cracks in the ice that form when ice floes diverge or shear as they move parallel to each other. The formation of leads is similar to mid-ocean ridges or shear zones that form from the earth's moving tectonic plates. The width of leads varies from a couple of meters to over a kilometer. Leads can often branch or intersect, creating a complex network of linear features in the ice. In the winter, leads begin to freeze almost immediately from the cold air." Natural Snow and Ice Data Center: https://nsidc.org/cryosphere/seaice/characteristics/leads.html

6. The Inuit Dog is not a breed of dog but an aboriginal landrace. The difference between a breed and a landrace is that pure breeds are genetically isolated from other breeds due to selective breeding. Poodles, for instance, have distinct characteristics that identify them as a breed that sets them apart from other kinds of dog. A landrace is a product of natural selection due to its isolation from other species. A landrace possesses certain traits that enable it to survive in its specific natural and cultural environment.

Chapter 6

1. Grasslands National Park is where sky meets prairie at the northern extension of the great plains. https://www.pc.gc.ca/en/pn-np/sk/grasslands

2. Badlands Wilderness Park is home to the largest deposits of dinosaur bones in the world. https://www.albertaparks.ca/albertaparksca/visit-our-parks/road-trips/canadian-badlands/

3. Painted Hills is known as one of the Seven Wonders of Oregon. It gets its name from the delicately colored stratifications of yellows, golds, blacks, and reds in the soil. These stratifications reveal

150

millions of years of history in the layers of the mountains, one color at a time. https://traveloregon.com/things-to-do/destinations/parks-forests-wildlife-areas/painted-hills/

4. Redwood National Park in California is home to the tallest and oldest trees on earth. It's a World Heritage Site and International Biosphere Reserve. https://www.visitredwoods.com/explore-the-redwoods/redwood-national-park/

5. Crater Lake National Park is the deepest lake in the USA and one of the most pristine on earth. https://www.nps.gov/crla/index.htm

Chapter 7

1. Sun Peaks Ski Resort is a family-friendly, all-season resort in British Columbia. https://www.sunpeaksresort.com/

Chapter 8

1. Giethoorn is a picturesque village in the province of Overijsel in Holland, known as Dutch Venice. https://www.nationalgeographic.com/travel/article/visit-giethoorn-quaint-village-without-cars.

2. Zerehi, Sima Sahar. CBC News. *Some kind of miracle: Friends of woman dying of cancer record album of her music.* https://www.cbc.ca/news/canada/north/woman-dying-cancer-records-album-1.3728861

Chapter 9

1. Helen Keller (1880-1968), author, disability rights advocate, lecturer. She lost her sight and hearing when she was 19 months old.

2. George, Jane. "Dying Iqaluit Woman's CD raises Funds for Nunavut Mental Health: Show Kindness, Do No Harm, Find

the Good." In: *Nunatsiaq News*. August 22, 2016. https://
nunatsiaq.com/stories/article/65674dying_iqaluit_womans_
CD_fundraises_for_Nunavut_mental_health/

Chapter 10

1. Rob Liano, author, business strategist, and motivational speaker.
    https://robliano.com/about/
2. Szczesniak, Daniel. "Missing You: 22 Honest Quotes about
    Grief." https://www.usurnsonline.com/grief-loss/missing-22-
    honest-quotes-grief/
3. Harvard Women's Health Watch. https://www.health.harvard.
    edu/heart-health/takotsubo-cardiomyopathy-broken-heart-
    syndrome

Chapter 11

1. Voltaire is the *nom de plume* or pen name of François Marie
    Arouet, a French writer, historian, and philosopher.
2. Semel Institute for Neuroscience and Human Behavior. *How Do
    You Cope?* https://www.semel.ucla.edu/dual-diagnosis-program/
    News_and_Resources/How_Do_You_Cope
3. Mayo Clinic Staff. "Exercise and Stress: Get moving to manage
    stress." https://www.mayoclinic.org/healthy-lifestyle/stress-
    management/in-depth/exercise-and-stress/art-20044469
4. Kessler, David. "I thought I knew everything about grief until my
    21-year-old son died." In: *The Irish Times*. March 18, 2021. https://
    www.irishtimes.com/culture/books/i-thought-i-knew-everything-
    about-grief-until-my-21-year-old-son-died-1.4060355

5. Dalai Lama XIV & Tutu, Desmond with Abrams, Douglas Carleton. *The Book of Joy: Lasting Happiness in a Changing World.* Viking. Penguin Random House Canada Ltd. 2016.

6. Forgeard, Marie J.C. "Perceiving Benefits after Adversity: The Relationship Between Self-reported Post-traumatic Growth and Creativity." In: *Psychology of Aesthetics, Creativity, and the Arts.* 2013, Vol. 7, No.3, 245-264. https://www.apa.org/pubs/journals/features/aca-a0031223.pdf

7. Basford, Johanna. *Secret Garden: An Inky Treasure Hunt and Coloring Book.* Laurence King Publishing Ltd. London. 2013.

8. Gilmore, Mikal, "The Life and Times of Bob Marley." In *Rolling Stone.* March 10, 2005. https://www.rollingstone.com/music/music-news/the-life-and-times-of-bob-marley-78392/

9. Zahed, Hyder. "The Power of Spoken Words." Updated, February 13, 2015. https://www.huffpost.com/entry/the-power-of-spoken-words_b_6324786

10. Murray, Bridget. "Writing to Heal." In: *American Psychological Association,* June 2002, Vol 33, No. 6. https://www.apa.org/monitor/jun02/writing

11. Kessler, David. https://www.davidkesslertraining.com/grief-journal-video

12. Kessler, David. *Finding Meaning: The Sixth Stage of Grief.* Simon & Schuster, 2020.

13. Stanborough, Rebecca Joy. "Benefits of reading books: How it can positively affect your life." In *Healthline,* October 15, 2019. https://www.healthline.com/health/benefits-of-reading-books#reduces-stress

14. Headley, C.W. The study found that 30 minutes of reading lowered blood pressure, heart rate, and feelings of psychological distress just as effectively as yoga and humor did. https://www.theladders.com/career-advice/study-people-that-engage-in-this-activity-daily-live-longer-and-feel-happier

15. Dalai Lama XIV & Tutu, Desmond with Abrams, Douglas Carleton. *The Book of Joy: Lasting Happiness in a Changing World.* Viking. Penguin Random House Canada Ltd. 2016.

16. Gilmore, Mikal. "The Life and Times of Bob Marley." In *Rolling Stone.* March 10, 2005. https://www.rollingstone.com/music/music-news/the-life-and-times-of-bob-marley-78392/

17. May, Gerald G. *The Wisdom of the Wilderness. Experiencing the Healing Power of Nature.* Harper One. New York. 2006.

18. Sheward, David. "7 Facts about Vincent van Gogh." In: Biography. Updated June 17, 2020. https://www.biography.com/news/vincent-van-gogh-biography-facts

19. Ottawa Regional Cancer Foundation. Maplesoft Jones Centre. 1500 Alta Vista Drive, Ottawa, ON, K1G 3Y9. Telephone: (613) 247-3527. https://www.ottawacancer.ca/how-can-we-help-you/cancer-coaching/

20. Churchill, Alexandra. "Tole Painting: The History Behind Collectible Folk-Art Treasures." https://www.marthastewart.com/1126615/tole-painting-collectible-folk-art-treasures

21. The Benefits of Laughter. https://www.helpguide.org/articles/mental-health/laughter-is-the-best-medicine.htm

22. Khajuria, Kavita MD. "Laughter is the Best Medicine." In: *Psychiatric Times. Vol. 35/8. August 17, 2018*

23. Salmansohn, Karen. In: AZ Quotes. https://www.azquotes.com/quote/1497190

24. Beck, Alan. "10 Ways Pets Support Mental Health." Newport Academy. https://www.newportacademy.com/resources/well-being/pets-and-mental-health/

Chapter 12

1. Mitch Albom is an American best-selling author and journalist. https://www.mitchalbom.com

2. Yellow birds. https://symbolismandmetaphor.com/yellow-bird-symbolism-meaning/

3. Warblers. https://www.auntyflo.com/magic/warbler

4. Ilisaqsivik Society. https://ilisaqsivik.ca/en/about/

5. Wounded Healers. https://www.youtube.com watch?v=ErLuPakgc1s

ABOUT THE AUTHOR

Kim Han is a retired librarian who worked on contract with the Canadian Embassy and a number of international organizations in the Netherlands. This included work in the Archives of the International Court of Justice, the judicial arm of the United Nations, where Kim conducted a feasibility study to justify the automation of the Court's antiquated records management system. She then accompanied her husband back home to Ottawa, Canada, upon his retirement and the birth of their first grandchild there.

Upon their return to Canada, rather than retiring, Kim chose to continue working in her fields of study. She worked as a substitute librarian at the Ottawa Public Library for 16 years and volunteered at the local hospital for more than 15. She has a Master's degree in German literature from Carleton University, as well as a Master in Library and Information Science from the University of Western Ontario.

Kim is fluent in English, German, Dutch and Indonesian. Kim also speaks French, although she says her French is not perfect.

Kim went parasailing in Bali when she was in her fifties and jumped off the Sky Tower in Auckland, New Zealand, the tallest free-standing structure in the Southern hemisphere, when she was 68 years old. Kim has lived in Indonesia, Germany, The Netherlands, and Canada, and traveled to six different continents. She enjoys cross-country skiing, canoeing, hiking, biking, and taking her dog, Parker, for walks to Beaver Pond near the retirement home where she and her husband moved in 2020.

Kim developed her love of writing when she worked on a bilingual children's television show for the CBC in Montreal. She has taken various writing workshops and written articles that were published in magazines and newspapers in Canada. Kim is the author of the book *The Canadian Inuit Dog: Icon of Canada's North* that she dedicated to her daughter, Siu-Ling. Siu-Ling lived in the Arctic, where she owned and ran a team of traditional Canadian Inuit Dogs.

Losing her daughter, Siu-Ling, to ovarian cancer was a devastating experience. Before that, Kim had to learn to live through the ups and downs of her daughter's thirteen-year cancer journey. How did she cope? How did she find the strength to carry on and find meaning in the most heart-wrenching pain for a parent to endure? In this book, Kim speaks from her heart as she shares how she learned to navigate through her grief journey to soothe the pain of her broken heart. It is her wish that you find inspiration and solace to help you through your own grief, one day at a time.

Besides Siu-Ling, Kim and Bing have two sons, Jeffrey and Timothy, granddaughter Kina in Ottawa and grandchildren Yi Zhen and Jin in London, UK.

ALSO BY KIM HAN

The Canadian Inuit Dog: Icon of Canada's North, Revodana Publishing, 2018.

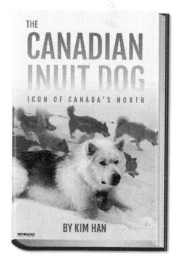

The proceeds of Siu-Ling's CD, "To Those Who Would Show Kindness" (https://siulingweb.wordpress.com/), and Kim's book, *The Canadian Inuit Dog: Icon of Canada's North* are being donated to Qimmivut and Wounded Healers, two programs of the Ilisaqsivik Society, a non-profit community-initiated and community-based Inuit organization and Canadian charity located in Clyde River, Nunavut, that is dedicated to the promotion of mental, physical, and spiritual healing and wellness in the community Siu-Ling loved.

Kim is a contributing author to two books:

Turning Point Moments: True Inspirational Stories About Creating a Life That Works for You. Compiled by Christine Kloser. Capucia Publishing. 2022.

Our Canada. Our Country. Our Stories: Inspirational Tales from the Heart and Soul of This Great Land. Reader's Digest Association of Canada. 2018.

Made in United States
Orlando, FL
11 April 2023

31993391R00096